Meaningful
WORK

Meaningful WORK

A Quest to Do Great Business,
Find Your Calling, and Feed Your Soul

Shawn Askinosie

with Lawren Askinosie

A TarcherPerigee Book

tarcherperigee

An imprint of Penguin Random House LLC
375 Hudson Street
New York, New York 10014

Most TarcherPerigee books are available at special quantity discounts
for bulk purchase for sales promotions, premiums, fund-raising, and educational needs.
Special books or book excerpts also can be created to fit specific needs.
For details, write: SpecialMarkets@penguinrandomhouse.com.

Library of Congress Cataloging-in-Publication Data

Names: Askinosie, Shawn, author. | Askinosie, Lawren, author.
Title: Meaningful work : a quest to do great business, find your calling, and
feed your soul / Shawn Askinosie, with Lawren Askinosie.
Description: New York, NY : TarcherPerigee, 2017.
Identifiers: LCCN 2017022703 | ISBN 9780143130314 (hardcover)
Subjects: LCSH: Job satisfaction. | Quality of work life. | Vocational guidance.
Classification: LCC HF5549.5.J63 A795 2017 | DDC 650.1—dc23
LC record available at https://lccn.loc.gov/2017022703

Printed in the United States of America
1   3   5   7   9   10   8   6   4   2

Book design by Elke Sigal

To my wife, Caron
—Shawn Askinosie

....

To my husband, Scott, and my friend Twabwike
—Lawren Askinosie

CONTENTS

CONTENTS

INTRODUCTION

What the hell am I doing here, I asked myself again. I'm neither Catholic nor a wilderness guy—by any stretch of the imagination. I parked and turned around to look in my backseat. I had packed all the requisite stuff: about fifteen books to keep me company, because I had never really been alone before, music, a candle, snacks. Of course, I brought my dog-eared and underlined *Tuesdays with Morrie,* the Bible, and my favorite Jimmy Carter book, *Sources of Strength.*

Assumption Abbey is a Trappist monastery that was established in 1950 by its mother house, the New Melleray Abbey in Iowa. A generous donor, inspired by Thomas Merton's *Seven Storey Mountain,* deeded three thousand acres in Missouri, surrounded by national forest land, to the monks. Still in the driver's seat, as though I was tethered, I reminded myself I was here for a retreat. And also for a special reason.

Arms full of aforementioned stuff, I found my way to the guesthouse. An Irish woman, Bridget, managed it in those days and she greeted me warmly. I think she sensed my uneasiness. There were just nine rooms in the guesthouse, she told me. As she led me down a corridor, she explained that, per my request, she had done her best to make sure that my room was the one in which my father had spent the last night of his life. Standing at the room's threshold, peering into its sparsely furnished interior, I felt a looming sense of dread coupled with a certainty that this weekend retreat at Assumption Abbey was exactly what I needed to be doing.

More than twenty-five years ago, I wore a suit and tie and stood by my mother's side next to my father's open casket at his visitation. I'd been to funerals before but I'd never stood next to a dead body for four hours. As everyone came through the line to offer their condolences and pearls of wisdom about how I needed to "be the man of the family," I remember robotically repeating: "I just don't know where I would be without my faith." I was fourteen.

During a break in the receiving line, Father Salman approached me. He was an Episcopal priest at our family's church, and my dad's good friend. I still remember his enveloping hugs. "Shawn, I want to tell you a story about what happened a few days ago at Assumption Abbey when I was with your dad on our men's retreat there." Preoccupied with feigning stoicism, I wasn't interested in listening, but I was a captive audience. "It was the last night that we were there and your father came across the hall and knocked on my door around 10:00 p.m. He said, 'Don, I was in my room praying. I wasn't dreaming. I was just visited by three angels. They told me that I was going to die, that I was going to be okay, and that my family would be protected.'"

He meant to comfort me, but instead I felt annoyed. Plain and simple, I wanted my dad back and the story of angels wasn't cutting it for me.

Person after person would shake my hand and tell me what a "great man" my dad was. They were right. My dad was a lawyer who fought for civil and criminal justice. I would often tag along with him to court and watch his trials. Among his many acts of community service, he started legal aid in our town for people who couldn't afford an attorney. He took me with him to the courthouse on Thursday nights and people would be lining a long hallway, waiting on wooden benches, to meet with him. Even though he was out of the Marines Corps by then, he always stayed in good shape, and taught boxing until he got sick. I remember him constantly doing one-handed push-ups. An extremely attentive father, he was the one to come into my room when nightmares struck. I remember the comforting glow of the dial on his Accutron Astronaut watch as he lay in bed with me while I tried to fall asleep.

When I was twelve he was diagnosed with lung cancer. He had not smoked since the military. He went to the Mayo Clinic for surgery and when he came home he and my mom said, "They got it all." They didn't.

Our family's faith was supposed to help us cope. I grew up Episcopalian, apparently an appealing denomination for a converted Jew (my dad) and former Southern Baptist (my mom). When my dad became sick we switched to a new church in town, St. James's Episcopal, considered the charismatic church, meaning the parishioners spoke in tongues, were filled with the Holy Spirit, and spoke prophetically in services. It kind of freaked me out. Convinced God would heal my dad if my family had the right kind of faith, the church prayer group would frequent our house for impromptu meetings where they'd lay hands on him. The prayer leader, an insurance salesman, would raise his voice at God and Satan during long, stressful sessions. Sometimes they'd stay for hours, doing things I didn't understand but definitely didn't find comforting. He and the others admonished me: "Don't talk to your dad about death. It is a sign of weakness and Jesus won't heal him if you have such doubt." So we didn't discuss it. My dad would try to talk to me, but I would say, "Dad we can't talk about it or you won't be healed."

There were more surgeries, and though they supposedly "got it all" each time, he kept getting sicker. His nausea was unrelenting, as was his excruciating pain, for which he needed multiple shots of Demerol throughout the day and night. We didn't have hospice care back then and my mom just couldn't bring herself to stick him with a needle. So the doctor taught me how to give my dad injections. I wanted to help relieve my hero's pain more than anything, and this was my chance. By thirteen, I was giving my dad several shots a day, often running out of healthy tissue on his hips. The smell of rubbing alcohol always brings these memories flooding back.

Cancer can be a roller coaster. Some days he felt great, and others, terrible. The week before he died, my dad tried a case in court. A few days later he made the trip to Assumption Abbey with his friends from church.

The day he returned from the abbey, Mother's Day 1975, he lay in bed most of the afternoon and evening, until about 10:30 p.m., when he called my mother upstairs. I went up to their room and he was sitting up on the side of the bed. He seemed confused and said, "I've always tried to help people." He lay back down and reached for a glass of water, and I asked him the question that had become my refrain over the past two years: "How are you feeling, Dad?" His reply was the same as always, "I'm feeling fine, son," even though he wasn't. They were the last words he spoke, to me or anyone. On his back, head on the pillow, he looked up and his eyes seemed to freeze in place. Time stopped and I screamed for God, "Please help me, please heal him! Please don't let him die!" over and over and over. I was desperate. My mom was crying hysterically and she went to close my little brother's bedroom door. I was afraid to touch him; he was dead, and there was nothing I could do. I have never in my life felt as overwhelmed by shock and sorrow as I did in that moment, or as helpless.

Within an hour the whole prayer group was at our house. Two ladies from the group asked me to come upstairs to my parents' bedroom, where my father's body still lay. We knelt down next to the bed and they tried to raise him from the dead back to life. After several minutes of this they told me that my dad did not want to come back, that they saw the blood come back to his lips but that he was happier now.

My father's death was, and remains, my greatest sorrow. During his military burial, two buglers played Echo Taps, one next to the casket and one unseen on the other side of National Cemetery. If I hear that melody today, I am right back there in the cemetery, as if it was just minutes ago. For the couple of years after his death, I waited to fit into his clothes, which still hung in the closet. I wanted to be able to wear his shoes. I wanted to keep his car, but my mom sold it. Though it was the right thing for her to do, I was pretty angry when she did it. We did not really talk much about my dad after he died.

As a kid, I was not equipped to grieve thoroughly. Instead, I told God I was going to prove that I didn't need Him and that I could accomplish all my goals without His help. Two years after my father died, when I was sixteen, I began working after school every day for a local lawyer, and I became Missouri Boys State governor. After that I qualified for the National Speech and Debate Tournament. While still in high school, I became a congressional page in the U.S. House of Representatives. After my freshman year in college, I volunteered for the American embassy in Thailand during the Vietnam refugee crisis. I subsequently spent a year of college in Japan. I maintained this pace into adulthood, keeping incredibly, sometimes manically, busy, usually with things that truly engaged me and that I felt good about doing.

Eventually, I became a successful criminal defense lawyer just like my dad. I spent the next two decades making money, winning seemingly impossible jury trials that were broadcast on Court TV, gaining prominence and recognition from national media outlets, and generally achieving things. Things I thought would make my dad proud. Things I thought I did without God.

Then, in 1999, I hit a roadblock. The stress and intensity of my work came to feel overwhelming. I became desperate to find a new path, though I had no idea what that might be. What I did know was that I could no longer continue to ignore the sorrow of my dad's sickness and death. Instead, I began a conversation with it.

I started by volunteering in the palliative care department at Mercy Hospital in my hometown. I was still trying cases, and I usually made time to visit the hospital on Fridays. The director of the program would give me a list of patients who'd asked for a visit, most of whom were at the end of life in some stage of dying. The patients were all over the hospital: ICU, Neuro, Cardiac, Oncology. I would stop by their rooms and talk to them about their younger days, their work, family, pie recipes, whatever they wanted. I would end my visit by asking if they'd like me to pray for them. To be clear, I wasn't there to "win souls" or make a spiritual cold call, but most patients who are in some stage of dying will take a prayer if offered. The interaction always deepened with the simple question: "What would you like me to pray for?" Some wanted to live two more weeks to celebrate their sixtieth wedding anniversary, some wanted relief from pain, some wanted healing, some wanted family restoration. I listened and I prayed their prayer. I would often ask them if I could hold their hand or touch their arm.

Let's face it: we spend most of our days thinking of... well... us. We think about ourselves a lot. I know I do. Those days at Mercy were some of the few moments in my life, really measured in seconds, where I thought about someone other than myself. These moments are rare and I encourage you to seek them out with all of your heart. Because I was serving these folks I was forced to be focused on them, not me.

The impact this had on me was enormous, and instantaneous. There were times after I'd completed my work at the hospital, while walking back to my car, that I was so filled with joy and light that it felt, quite literally, like my feet weren't touching the ground. Like I was where I was supposed to be, in the moment I was supposed to be there.

Of course, that lighter-than-air feeling would dwindle the further I got from the hospital, especially when I was at work. It would take another five years to determine what bigger changes I wanted to make in my life. It's a funny paradox, but the first step in sorting myself out was actually not to think about myself, and instead to focus on other people.

Kahlil Gibran wrote, "Our greatest joy is sorrow unmasked." It took me twenty-five years to figure that out. Gibran understood that joy can be found, and if not found then cultivated, via a deep acknowledgment of our sorrows. He knew that the exploration of heartbreak—our own, and the world's—leads to an expansive understanding of our true self. He knew that there, we can create meaning.

I started a small-batch chocolate factory at the forefront of the American craft chocolate boom. We practice direct trade, open-book management, and reverse scale, which are integral to our business model—and, I'm willing to bet, applicable to yours. It's in these and other collaborative, humane approaches to business that I have found immeasurable meaning. (Also in the delicious chocolate we make!) By establishing close, just, trusting relationships with everyone with whom we do business, my team and I find a deep sense of purpose, and terrific pleasure, in our work. These days I spend my time operating the business and traveling frequently. When I'm not in Ecuador, Tanzania, or the Philippines working with our farmer partners, I'm meeting with our retailers, schools, and other organizations across the globe to share our story and unique business model—and of course sample chocolate.

My exploration of my deepest sorrow allowed me to uncover passions I didn't know I had. Ultimately, it led me to the discovery of my vocation, and to the creation of Askinosie Chocolate.

Like everyone, I'm flawed, and often confused. There have been periods of my life where I pushed through, where I kept it all together and the outside world thought I was untouchable. And there came a time when I couldn't do it anymore.

Then there are times like now, when I can feel the earth firmly under my feet; when I am unsure about what chocolate problems the next day may bring, but I feel confident and purposeful in the present moment.

This book is for entrepreneurs at heart or in practice—or both. It is for those who are searching for their own personal meaning in their work, and seeking to transform that meaning into a vocation. Whether you're beginning a new venture or want to infuse your current one with dedicated purpose, my hope is that my experiences, and the deep and enduring lessons I've learned from them, will help you find your own business vocation. I hope your copy of this book will become dog-eared, with notes and marks in the margins, because it's inspired an idea of what *your* next step is for you and your business.

At the end of each chapter, you'll find exercises to aid you in honing your personal vocation and translating that into a business vocation. You will learn how to host a vocation summit at your organization. You'll also learn how to use a tool called "visioning." I've been using it for many years now, for projects big and small. I wish I had known of it when I began the factory, but since then I've created a vision for Askinosie Chocolate and it's helped me and my team to make good decisions: how to determine, for instance, which opportunities to take, and which to decline because they're ultimately not a good fit; how to assess whether the steps we're taking now are leading us to where we aim to be as a company in the future. Visioning is a practice I learned from my good friend and mentor, Ari Weinzweig, of the beloved Zingerman's in Ann Arbor. I've adapted his visioning model slightly and now teach it to various businesses, schools, and even Tanzanian children and cocoa farmers (more on that later).

In the bigger picture, I hope the story of our company can serve as a little light that will shine into people's hearts—including further into my own, my colleagues', and our farmer partners'—so that many more of us will actively transform the world, day by day, with meaningful work that allows us all to become truer and truer versions of ourselves. Together, maybe we can become beacons for the future of capitalism.

Looking back to that fateful day at Assumption Abbey, the first day of my first retreat there, I had no idea it was the first day of dozens of retreats, or the first day of my journey to becoming a family brother there. And I certainly didn't know it was the first day of my path to a new vocation, a vocation involving bean-to-bar chocolate making and cocoa farmers in far-flung corners of the earth.

The place where angels visited my father on his last night of life is not sorrowful at all, but one of joy and peace—I just had to go and meet it to uncover that fact. I hope you'll join me on this journey of meeting your sorrows head-on, finding yourself in the service of others, and creating the fulfilling work life you've dreamed of along the way.

Have a question about something in the book? I may not have the answers, but sometimes I'm good for a laugh. Feel free to e-mail me at hello@shawnaskinosie.com.

....

CHAPTER 1

Find Meaning in Your Work, or Else It Just Might Kill You

I've known my friend Danny since childhood. He helped me study for the Missouri bar exam in 1992. He was a brilliant whirlwind of a lawyer who specialized in mass tort litigation, mostly what are called "toxic torts," like defective drugs that end up hurting and killing people.

He made a lot of money; I mean a lot of money. He also medicated himself with alcohol in the process. On the outside, Danny was winning. Danny the person, though, was rudderless, in pain, and without a vocation.

After almost twenty years of representing plaintiffs, winning cases, and pounding on other lawyers, Danny left the law. And do you want to know what he did next? He helped his wife start a scrapbooking business. He immersed himself in colored paper, holiday stencils, adhesive dots, and craft rubber stamps. He wanted to serve Nikki in pursuit of her passion and that's exactly what he did for four years. Unfortunately the business went south, and they moved to another city, where Nikki found a great new job.

Years earlier, while in the process of getting sober, Danny had attended a workshop that helped people discover a better version of themselves. Because he found them beneficial, he continued attending these courses over the next several years, as an assistant, while he phased out of law and into scrapbooking.

Eventually he began training to become a paid teacher of these workshops. Danny never considered that it could be a career, until he started working with Nikki. That's where the mystery of service and vocation comes into focus: while he was serving his wife—not thinking about himself—space was created for him to consider this new career, a life of helping others, with the skills he'd learned over the previous decade of workshops and training.

Danny's selfless service to Nikki was ultimately how he found himself; and importantly, it was a bridge to his vocation.

When I asked Danny to describe this, he said, "I discovered that one of my core values was kindness, in a way that on my deathbed it will matter to me: was I kind? The courtroom was no longer a place for me to live that core value." Today he travels the country leading workshops for people from all walks of life, from Orthodox Jewish teens in New York City to middle schoolers in San Diego, to LAPD gang unit cops, to people simply searching for a better life in St. Louis. He has a thriving coaching practice and makes, in his exact words, "a whole f—ing lot less" than his days as a lawyer, but he loves his life.

I've seen him at work and if there was ever a person who dodged death by finding and living out their vocation, it's my friend Danny.

Like Law for Chocolate

"Why did you quit law?"

"Why on earth chocolate?"

And my personal favorite: "I bet this career is a lot sweeter than your old one, huh?"

It's possible I've told my lawyer-to-chocolate-maker story a thousand times in the past ten years in response to those questions. From college campuses to boardrooms to tours of our chocolate factory, these are the most common questions I'm asked. And I get it. People want to know how and why I made this crazy leap. They also want to know how I manage to "do it all." How our team of sixteen people, working on a humble street in a small city in the Midwest, makes chocolate that wins awards around the world. Or how we practice direct trade with smallholder farmers across the globe. Or how our small chocolate factory is able to feed thousands of students per day in Tanzania and the Philippines with no donations. After hearing me speak, a lot of folks say—either with excitement or despair—that they wish they could do what I'm doing, but don't know how or where to start or that it all seems too daunting. I like to answer their questions with as much detail as time permits; the good, the bad, and the ugly. And my reply always centers around the fact that Askinosie Chocolate is my vocation and it's the only reason we're able to do what we do.

ASKINOSIE CHOCOLATE TOUCHSTONE: DIRECT TRADE

We've been directly trading with cocoa farmers around the world since the beginning. This means we not only pay a premium for our cocoa beans, but we personally travel to each of our origin communities—Ecuador, Tanzania, and the Philippines—yearly. On these trips, I inspect our crop of beans to ensure they meet the specifications outlined in our contract. We share profits, in cash, based on a percentage of sales of the previous year's crop of cocoa beans. We translate our financials into the farmers' language and walk through it line by line, to show how we arrived at the calculation. We tour the small family farms and we discuss the health of their cacao trees; we talk about postharvest and fermentation techniques. We'll roast freshly dried cocoa beans together over a fire to analyze their flavor. And I always bring chocolate for us all to taste, including bars made from their cocoa beans as well as our other origins. Direct trade is about relationships. It's a practice, and a way of being.

It's not as simple as "Follow your dream," which is nice, if trite, and also not that helpful. How exactly do you follow your dream? What does that look like? What are the next steps? In this chapter, I provide an alternative to this platitude by suggesting some answers to these very questions. I hope the lessons I've learned and the mistakes I've made along this path to my vocation inspire you to find meaning in your work. But before we discuss your business we need to talk about *you*. You have to find your personal vocation. I encourage you to follow these steps, try some of the exercises at the end of the chapter, and then go live what comes out of it.

For the record: no, making chocolate is not necessarily "sweeter" than my former life as a lawyer. Try standing at the counsel table in the well of a courtroom, shoulder to shoulder with a client—in whose innocence you believe with every fiber of your being, but who is charged with murder and might die by lethal injection—as the jury files in, the foreperson says they have reached a verdict, and the words "not guilty" are read by the judge in slow motion. Is that "sweet"? No, not exactly. But it sure is gratifying, gut-wrenching, and life affirming. Nevertheless, chocolate is what I do now and it, too, has its gratifying, gut-wrenching, life-affirming moments.

Vocation, Vocation, Vocation

My grandparents lived on the same farm in Miller, Missouri, for over sixty-five years. I think they left the state once to go with my parents, my brother, and I to Panama City Beach in 1972 (the entire trip they fretted about their animals and the weather back home). Their daily schedule was waking before the sun to milk the cows, collect the eggs, eat, tend the garden, work the fields, eat, work the fields some more, milk the cows, eat and then to bed, wake up, and repeat. I love the monastic rhythm of that work now, but I didn't appreciate it as a boy. It was boring and I didn't like helping with chores. It always seemed too hot or too cold.

But the farming life was their vocation. They were called to it and clearly loved it, all of it. The best expression of my grandmother's vocation is how she treated people who visited the farm. Everyone left with some kind of food that she had baked, canned, or picked from the garden. She insisted on it.

In South America they call it a *plan de vida*; in Japan, *ikigai*. I call it vocation—the reason you do what you do. We all need a reason to live, a reason to wake up in the morning. My grandparents woke up in the morning to grow and harvest food to nourish people. This reason for being can be cultivated in your personal life. But it's also entirely possible to create it with your work. In fact, not only is it possible, it's essential. After all, according to the math people, we spend approximately eighty thousand hours of our lifetime at work. You better hope your work fulfills you, or at the very least is enjoyable.

If you follow the advice in this book, I promise you will find some things out about yourself. My hope is that you'll uncover your personal vocation, and apply that to your business. This is not only the best way to achieve the fulfillment you seek but it's the best way to create a successful, sustainable organization. The impact of vocation reverberates throughout your life, both internally and externally, your business, your community, and the world by allowing you to realize your true self and by meeting and serving the needs of others.

Most people find it easy to recognize when something needs to change in themselves or their business, but knowing what to do about it is another matter. So many people share with me how miserable and unfulfilled they are—they know they want their work to look and feel different, but they have no concept of what to do to find out *what* that should be. In this chapter, I will explain how I did it; it begins with finding your personal vocation. Chapter 2 is about honing your business vocation, and while your instinct may be to skip this stuff about personal vocation, I urge you not to, because your personal vocation will lead you to your business vocation. You can sell your company and start a new one, or buy a franchise now, you can quit your job and search for another, but if you don't figure things out before you move on, you'll almost certainly find yourself in the same spot. You will not find meaning in the new work just because it's different. For some entrepreneurs this will be a painful chapter, but I ask you to bear with me and give it considerable thought, reflection, and work.

Time for a Change

I never lost a criminal jury trial. I am one of a handful of lawyers in the country who have successfully obtained a not-guilty verdict in a death penalty case. My reputation as an overprepared and aggressive criminal defense attorney was built on murder cases. Once, I had prepared so many D-ring binders that I had to rent a U-Haul trailer to drive them to the courthouse. The D-ring binders, themselves, were a source of stress for the state's expert witnesses. They made a distinct sound when I opened them up, a metallic thud. The witnesses eventually knew that when I opened a binder it was to show them a document, usually one they had authored, and that they were lying. The sound of my binder opening often caused a visible flinch. It reminded me of Pavlov's dogs.

I've crawled on my hands and knees at night, in the dark, at a crime scene to see blood spatter patterns glow with luminol. I've been to an autopsy and smelled bone dust. I've used microscopic evidence with

DNA material to free a man convicted of a rape he did not commit after serving two years in solitary confinement on a sentence of seventy years. I've had death threats. The most bizarre was when someone chopped up a deer and smeared blood all over the front porch of my law office building. It never really bothered me until my family was threatened, too. That was when my wife (who hates guns) and I took tactical handgun classes. I went a step further with low-light handgun training. It got so serious, we eventually had a security expert come out to our house to practice and plan what-ifs in the event of a hostage scenario. This was when my daughter, Lawren—incidentally, a great contributor to this book—was a young girl, so we wanted to be very careful.

I loved my work, despite the sadness surrounding much of it, until I didn't.

There was one particular moment in my law career when I knew it was time to pivot and begin looking for another dream. I was representing a client named Debbie. Debbie believed, supported by evidence, that her ex-husband was sexually molesting their young daughter. For years Debbie had successfully convinced the courts to keep him away from her. Then one day a court decided, despite Debbie's valiant efforts, to allow the ex-husband his first unsupervised visit with her child in years. The day before the planned visit, Debbie, believing her daughter was about to suffer a fate worse than death, gave her a sleeping pill, carried her to the car, turned it on, closed the garage door, and let it run with the two of them inside.

When the police found them the child was dead and Debbie was near death and unconscious. She had hoped to die with her daughter. She was rushed by helicopter to another city, where she was placed in a hyperbaric oxygen chamber. When she woke up she was immediately charged with first-degree murder. The family hired me to defend her. It was a no-win case. A loss would mean that she might spend the rest of her life in prison. The absolute best I could hope for was lifetime commitment to a state mental hospital. I pled her "not guilty by reason of mental disease or defect," otherwise known as the insanity defense. Guess how many times that defense has worked in the United States? Not very many. Basically never.

This trial was particularly brutal. Due to heavy media coverage, the jury was sequestered in a nearby hotel and instructed to have no contact with the outside world. The judge and I clashed at every stage of the case.

Minutes before my opening statement was set to begin, the judge let the prosecutor mark all over my integral (not to mention expensive) exhibit with a black Sharpie. Boiling over, I remember exactly what I blurted out: "Well, Judge, why don't you just go ahead and stick a needle in her arm now and get it over with." He threatened to hold me in contempt and put me in jail if I made one more statement like that. The judge repeatedly attempted to prevent me from getting into evidence why she did what she did: that she believed her ex-husband was sexually abusing her daughter. And unfortunately there was a mountain of evidence to support her belief. It was totally relevant. But before the trial the judge ruled that evidence inadmissible. Midtrial, I appealed that decision to a higher court with no luck. So I pushed and pushed and pushed again. My job was to make a record of any possible error in the trial, so that there was a chance the case could be reversed at a higher level and sent back for a retrial. I deeply believed that not letting the jury consider that evidence was a mistake and I just couldn't let it go.

Right before closing arguments, the judge called me and the prosecutor into his chambers. He calmly explained his decision, one that is so rare it almost never happens in civil or criminal law. He told us, "I've been listening to the evidence this whole trial and I've decided I am taking it away from the jury because I believe that she did not know the wrongfulness of her conduct. I believe the state's expert." He believed my cross-examination of the state's own expert. I was astonished. He continued, "Here is what we are going to do. You, Mr. Prosecutor, are going to let her plead down to second-degree murder and I am going to put her on five years' probation [the max for a felony in Missouri]. Shawn, go out and talk to your client."

I was already nearly numb from the trial, emotionally drained and physically exhausted. For a moment I sat there in utter disbelief; I'd not contemplated a win of this magnitude as being even remotely possible. People charged with first-degree murder don't get probation. She was going to walk out of the courthouse, tormented but free.

I left the judge's chambers and met with Debbie in the anteroom off the main courtroom. Still in shock, I explained to her what the judge had said and what he was proposing. As I was talking to her something happened that had never once, in any of my time practicing law, happened: I began to cry. Debbie hugged me and told me that it was over, that I'd done a good job. My client, who would have rather been dead and with her daughter than living on earth, was comforting me. That is not the way it's supposed to be. *I am the comforter, not the comforted,* I admonished myself.

In that moment, I felt a huge shift inside, though I didn't know exactly what it meant at the time. On some level, way down deep, I knew then that it was over—that however much I'd loved my career, I probably couldn't do it anymore. But it took a while longer for that knowledge to bubble to the surface.

Meanwhile, of course, I did some stupid stuff first to assuage my discomfort, like buying a convertible Mercedes. What a novel idea! I sold it four months later. I also tried other areas of the law and, while challenging, I could tell it was not helping. I continued to practice with great success and there were many days when I knew I was in the right place, advocating for the accused. I had always loved the courtroom and preparing for the courtroom, especially cross-examination. But at some point during those uncertain years, I stopped loving it. This was uncomfortable and for a long time I struggled against this truth, grasping at anything I could control and then squeezing it too tightly.

The stress and discomfort began to manifest themselves physically. One day I had some chest pains and went to my doctor, who sent me to the hospital for an overnight stay. It turned out there was no problem with my heart, so I was sent to a psychologist. I occasionally had little panic attacks, manifesting as a punch to my sternum, though I did not know what they were at the time. Finally, I ended up with something similar to chronic fatigue syndrome, necessitating regular checkups with a neurologist for three years. All of the physical symptoms dovetailed with my fear of death and I ended up on antidepressants. They helped some, but by then I could see that my body was literally telling me I needed a change. Eventually I could no longer ignore the nagging feeling that I needed a totally new inspiration—and vocation (I didn't call it that at the time). So I began searching in earnest.

Get Woke

As I've reflected on Debbie's case over the years, it's clear that that conversation with her in the anteroom at the courthouse was the pivotal moment when my life shifted. We all have these moments, but the key is the degree to which we are awake enough to see them. The more awake we are, the greater the chance of seeing it. Conversely, the more asleep we are, the bigger the moment might have to be to receive our attention. I was fast asleep, like, in-the-middle-of-a-REM-cycle asleep.

Once I had accepted that I needed to leave law, I prayed a very simple prayer: "Dear God, please give me something else to do." I prayed it every day, usually repeating it throughout the day. I had no idea just how long I would pray that prayer. It turned out to be five years. To be clear: I wasn't following a dream at that time; I was just praying to escape my old one. I didn't have a new dream yet. It just became obvious that no amount of talk therapy or dosage change in my Lexapro was going to keep me practicing law.

I want to share the process of how I uncovered my personal vocation—and meaning in my work—with you here. You'll also find some exercises at the end of this chapter to help you get started.

STEPS TO UNCOVER YOUR PERSONAL VOCATION

Step 1: Don't try to find it by endless research.

Step 2: Inventory your talents, your passion, and what the world needs.

Step 3: Begin with your sorrow.

Step 4: Serve selflessly.

Step 5: Expect nothing in return.

Step 6: Discover the internal space where you can ponder your next steps with clarity.

Step 1: Don't Try to Find It by Endless Research

It's tempting to type into a search bar, "What should I do with my life?" and maybe some of you have (full disclosure: I did). For all of us type A, hard-charging, overachieving doers and seekers the pattern begins with researching the hell out of whatever it might be. This often means hours, days, or weeks of screen time. In my experience, this research takes two tracks: *how* do I find the next thing/inspiration/vocation and *what* should it be? We pore over books, blogs, podcasts, Facebook, and LinkedIn, and we talk to our family and friends about all of it. Then, if you're like me, you seek out experts and get their feedback on your ideas for the next big thing in your life. I did all of this for a very long time. If you do it, too, my advice is to stop it.

The problem? This research is a detrimental feedback loop, each "answer" only leading to more questions until you finally reach a new level of Dante's Inferno. This research often leads to paralysis, when what we really need is action. Reading about and listening to something does not make it happen, despite our intense efforts to the contrary. Even if we are the most disciplined students of [fill-in-the-blank subject] there's still that pesky thing called action. I read about meditation consistently and I listen to podcasts about it a few times per month, but it does not make me a more dedicated—or better—meditator. It doesn't even cause me to meditate more.

I spent about five years researching, talking, and praying before I arrived at chocolate. I was looking for a spark, a light, a jolt, or maybe a voice that would say, "This—is—it!" and it never happened. The more desperate I grew, the further it traveled away from me. My frustration magnified and it probably caused more depression and anxiety. I told myself that I was the best investigator I knew, the guy who'd built a name on leaving no stone unturned—and yet I couldn't break this code! What I needed was space, clarity, and peace and what I created for myself was clutter, confusion, and chaos. At the end of the chapter, I'll give you an exercise—to fill up the time you used to spend Googling!—to help you find that mental calm.

Step 2: Inventory Your Talents, Your Passion, and What the World Needs

If you Google "vocation" (but again: don't!) the first couple of pages of results reflect the Catholic evolution of the word. But vocation isn't inherently religious; in fact, it does not have to be religious at all. The Trappist monk Thomas Merton, my favorite Catholic writer, said this about discerning vocation:

> Discovering vocation does not mean scrambling toward some prize just beyond my reach but accepting the treasure of true self I already possess. Vocation does not come from a voice "out

there" calling me to be something I am not. It comes from a voice "in here" calling me to be the person I was born to be, to fulfill the original selfhood given me at birth by God.

Our vocation is right here, within us, and we have the power, only if we can hear our own voice calling us, to become our true self. Becoming our true self is hard work, though. It is for me. It's also an ongoing process.

What is the intersection of your talents, what the world needs, and your passion? You can draw a Venn diagram or an idea map or you can write out a list. Remember that this exercise defines vocation but does not tell you how to get there. That comes later. While you're working on this exercise, keep in mind that we're not just talking about leaving the work you're doing and forging a new path. We're also considering the possibility of forging a new path right where you are.

Let's begin by listing your talents. You could also look at these as your skill set. If you've lived very long at all, this is not a short list. I know Malcolm Gladwell says you can practice your drum grooves for ten thousand hours and then sub in for Questlove on *The Tonight Show*. Can we set that aside for just a bit, though? Becoming Questlove might be your dream, but we need to stay grounded. Is it within the realm of reason? That's where we will start.

A list of my talents and skills would have actually been a short list: I was really good at cross-examining witnesses in criminal trials; I was even better at cross-examining expert witnesses; and my ultimate skill was cross-examining a lying law enforcement officer. Awesome. Those skills are totally universally transferable to a plethora of next career choices (not). More generally, I understood how to craft a defense, how to tell a story, and how to create reasonable doubt. That basically intersects with nothing and it was no longer my passion. I didn't have a degree in business, had taken zero accounting classes, had no experience in manufacturing, was not mechanical, and wasn't really that great with numbers. Sounds like the recipe for a fantastic leader of a manufacturing business, right? I did have a few transferable talents, though, like crafting and telling stories (marketing), locating difficult-to-find people (excellent cocoa farmers), and solving complex problems (manufacturing and international business).

Now let's tackle the planet's needs. Sitting down and listing all of them isn't much help because you'd never stop writing. Instead, it's ideal to reflect upon this question with regard to the talents you've already noted. "What does the world need?" is an important question as it relates to this exercise because if you're skilled at and passionate about something but the world does not require it, then there could be a problem. You might be great at making fur sinks or electric dog polishers (thank you, Steve Martin, for those examples of useless appliances), but does the world need those things? Also, we are not talking about the Steve Jobs scenario in which you teach the world to rely on the thing you will make or service you provide. The path to vocation is smoother if we can survey the landscape in our neighborhood, workplace, city, or world at large and take stock of existing needs. (This is a great place for me to point out that I have a liberal view when it comes to needs of the world.)

Does the world "need" the best morning bun? Liz Prueitt, cofounder of Tartine Bakery of San Francisco, makes the most delicious morning buns I've ever eaten, and I can personally testify that the world needs them. Is her bakery meeting a "need" of her community or the world? I don't know the answer to that question (however, I would argue that yes, she is providing a social benefit to the world), but either way what matters most is that Liz cares about her craft. And the world does need talented, thoughtful craftspeople. Although she and her company exemplify social consciousness, that fact in itself doesn't legitimize her morning buns (and pretty much everything else she and her husband, Chad, make).

My point is that you will be best served in this exercise if you think about the world's needs with a wide-angle lens. Don't discount an idea you have merely because it's not about feeding hungry children. We all benefit when people pursue excellence—that in and of itself is meeting a need. Another way of looking at this exercise is that once your vocation ideas come into sharper focus you will readdress this question and ask with your vocation in mind, "Does the world need this?" Human connection and joy are embedded in the pursuit of excellence as a vocation. Without them, you might have a fine product but one that's lacking meaning. I am certain that Liz Prueitt contemplates her heart connection to the people who enjoy her morning buns, whether for the first or the five-hundredth time.

Finally, you need to consider your passions. What are they? How do they tie in? Pondering this matter requires clarity, and in some cases vulnerability, because we need to be honest with ourselves.

The purpose of step 2 is only to make the lists/diagrams/charts—that's it. Make it, review it, meditate on it, and then set it aside. You'll come back to this document only after you've started living all of the ideas of these steps. Or, paradoxically, you may never come back to it. Then why go to the trouble of writing it down? Because it's important to get it out of your brain, on paper, and ready for easy reflection and discussion if needed.

Step 3: Begin with Your Sorrow

We've talked about where *not* to look, and we've made an inventory of your talents, the needs of the world, your passion, and the resulting intersections. Now the real work begins. Here we will confront and befriend your sorrows.

The next few steps will help you find the bridge to your vocation. Action-oriented entrepreneurs need this particular step in the worst way. This step also can and should be repeated over and over throughout life. It's not easy or, usually, pleasant, but each time I acknowledge my sorrows I learn something valuable about myself. I strongly encourage those of us who struggle with overresearch and overaction to not skip this step. You know who you are.

Let's return to Gibran's words: "Your joy is your sorrow unmasked." He adds, "The deeper that sorrow carves into your being, the more joy you can contain." Indeed, on the other side of our sorrow lives our joy. My grief over my dad's death ran deep and I am living proof that great joy is inextricably tied to it. Uncovering this sorrow ultimately led me to the creation of Askinosie Chocolate.

For many, visiting these sorrows is so painful it's to be avoided at all cost. However, we cannot be inoculated against sorrow. If we live long enough we will experience it. But the reality is very few will do the gut-wrenching work discussed here. I've heard lots of people say, "Well, that *was* my sorrow but not anymore. I'm over it." Being "over" a sorrow does not mean its impact has been removed. It still happened; it still helped shape you. In one of the exercises at the end of this chapter I am going to ask you: what are your sorrows? Most people find this examination of grief frightening—and that's completely understandable. Before we've looked it in the eye, our own sorrow is like the dragon hiding in the cave. Think of yourself as on the hero's journey to face the dragon. It takes hard work to locate it, and courage to enter its cave.

Even if you've already healed, and developed a healthy perspective on your sorrow, the fact remains that it holds the key to great joy and is therefore worth returning to.

Once you've acknowledged and explored your sorrow, you are ready to contemplate how the seeds of joy might be discovered in that same emotional space. I always recommend some sort of service. For many, the most rewarding "place" of service involves human contact and the chance for emotional connection. During my search for meaning, I cofounded Lost & Found, a grief center for children and teens who've experienced the death of a loved one, with my friend Dr. Karen Scott. In seventeen years we've served thousands of young people and their families, helping them remember, survive remembering, and possibly find joy in their remembrance as well. I helped facilitate our first group of teens whose parents had died of cancer, from an accident, or by suicide. This work remains my joy, the other side of my sorrow, to this day.

I recall one middle school boy whose mother had died of breast cancer. He'd been a linebacker on the football team, and quite good at it. But he quit the team after she died, because he could remember her voice cheering him on from the stands, and it was too painful. After he'd been in our group for nearly two years he started playing football again and enjoying it. He asked me to come to a game. I'll never forget watching him play. I don't remember if they won or lost, but I was so joyful for him, that he was healing and learning to enjoy his life again.

It's important to understand that this is a process that never ends. I recently started facilitating a teen group again, a new one we started last year for children and teens whose parents are in the midst of a life-threatening illness. I was afraid during the lead-up to our first group night. It's one thing to work with kids after the death of a parent but quite another to work with them while their parent is sick. I felt as if I was putting my head into the mouth of a lion. Once we got started, though, it was great, and most important, it seems to make a difference to the kids. Anyway, my point is that service is not a final destination. We can keep returning to it, again and again.

Step 4: Serve Selflessly

Writing a check to your favorite charity is great, but that's not what I'm referring to here. Nor am I talking about joining the board of that charity, or even starting your own nonprofit.

As mentioned, while I was searching for my next path I started volunteering in the palliative care department at a local hospital. I treasure this experience. It was a catalyst for me.

Where and who may act as this catalyst for you? Where is the place that you can serve? This work will have an astronomically high return on investment. Obviously those you serve benefit from your service, but good things happen for you as well. Of course, it's possible that you will decide that this service is "it" for you and you need not look further for vocation. It's more likely, though, that this can be a bridge for you as it was for me. For the first time in my life I found joy transformed from my greatest sorrow. And I also found my true self.

Step 5: Expect Nothing in Return

Taking a "step" is not always a concrete action you can point to, though we want it to be; I've learned that the hard way over the years. I know that the reasons for doing this work are not always evident. Sometimes it may even feel pointless. And in fact, that very elusiveness is central to this next step, which is to continue opening your heart to the world's needs, with no expectation of profit or benefit. Gandhi said, "The best way to find yourself is to lose yourself in the service of others." Jesus was getting at something similar when he said, "Take up your cross and follow me." Morrie Schwartz, of *Tuesdays with Morrie*, said, "When you learn how to die you learn how to live." They're all saying, In order to live, you must let go of yourself.

This service I am speaking of is not a weekend peak experience in which you'll emerge on Sunday after encountering a burning bush, walk down from the mountain, and proclaim the new path of your life.

In my case, the work at Mercy was years long. While doing this work I continued to actively practice law, fruitlessly search online for my next path, and seek out contemplative prayer at home and the abbey. It's also important to point out that I didn't feel well during this time. I was fatigued for a few years and experienced episodes of severe brain fog. I was on and off antidepressants, trying to get some relief. The sustained work at the hospital, week after week, gave me moments of not thinking about myself. It was the true bridge to my vocation because of what happened in the next step. This service can be your bridge to your true vocation, too.

It's good to dwell in this step and do the work without expectation of anything at all. After a few weeks, it's okay to have expectations. But suspending expectations for even a few seconds will be tough. My technique was to take a few minutes before visiting patients to go to the hospital chapel to center myself. I prayed briefly for the group I was about to visit and for myself; that I could suspend my ego and what Buddhist thinkers often refer to as "monkey mind"—that constant "What's in it for me?" mental chatter—for just a bit. On many days I also stopped by the chapel at the conclusion of my day for a moment of thanks.

Step 6: Discover the Internal Space Where You Can Ponder Your Next Steps with Clarity

I believe those of us who are really stuck, struggling and fighting to find the next path, require a more dramatic meeting of our sorrow and joy. Mine was admittedly Shakespearean: going to a hospital and visiting dying people when my greatest sorrow was my dad's death.

It was this place, of not thinking of myself for a few seconds, where the space was created for me to be open and listen. This is the great paradox, the mystery: when you immerse yourself in serving others wholeheartedly you find yourself, along with many answers to the "what next" questions you've been seeking. This time away from obsessing about how unhappy I was in my career, and how bad I felt physically, and what my next move should be, allowed me the space I needed to have true clarity. It was as if someone was wiping the fog off the windshield of my mind and I could finally see the path ahead.

I didn't know it at the time, but it was this space that allowed me to be the real Shawn—and to consider the idea of making chocolate. It came to me one day when I was driving alone to the funeral of my mother's elderly cousin Maxine. The services were held at Grays Point Cemetery near my grandparents' old farm.

A couple of years earlier, I'd bought a Big Green Egg and started grilling. Then I started baking and making chocolate desserts. I knew that I loved food and thought perhaps my next passion would somehow relate to that. On my way to the funeral the thought just popped into my mind: "How about making chocolate from scratch?" I had no idea what "from scratch" meant, zero idea that chocolate came from a bean. But within three months, I was in the Amazon learning how farmers influence the flavor of a cocoa bean by how they harvest their crops.

The farming aspect of it was fortuitous. I had long felt connected to farming because of my grandparents. I've mentioned that I spent a lot of time with them growing up. Their needs were simple. They were kind. Neither was educated beyond the sixth or seventh grade. They worked very hard and never complained. They loved my brother and me immensely. Growing up, I got tired of going to the farm and wanted to stay close to my friends and so I pushed them away a little. Once in college, I pushed away even more. I was thirty-three when they both died within six months of each other after sixty-five years of marriage. In my forties I started to really comprehend who they were. I don't put them on pedestals, but I hold them in my heart as models of wisdom, joy, hard work, kindness, and peacefulness. What does this have to do with cocoa farmers? Everything! I carry a sorrow around connected to my grandma and grandpa, and working with cocoa farmers gives me a pathway to joy.

At the beginning of the chapter I said that your vocation may well lie at the intersection of your talents, what the world needs, and your passion. This is how I found my elusive passion, the inspiration for my current chocolate vocation. It's like trying to grab smoke. The harder I tried, the more difficult the process. Once I focused on true service— not myself—it seemed easier to stand in the smoke and let it rest on me without me having to grab it so desperately. That's my best attempt to explain an unexplainable mystery.

The Point of No Return

As I was beginning my chocolate business, I was also winding down my law practice with the help of my great friend and law partner, Stacie.

She began taking over my caseload while I began figuring out how the hell to start a chocolate factory. You always hear about the "point of no return": you've taken a deep breath, made a decision, and ventured down the path only to realize there's really not a great way to turn around without paddling upstream. My deep-breath-and-decision was buying a rebuilt hundred-year-old granite mill, called a *melangeur*, from Germany. It weighed six thousand pounds and I had no place to store such a thing at my house or law office, so I bought a building.

I take great comfort from something the novelist Antoine de Saint-Exupéry said: "What saves a man is to take a step. Then another step." I repeat it to myself when doubt creeps in—which it inevitably does, at least once in a while. Then you keep going. And it's almost always worth it. If I had known all of the personal and professional challenges of starting a chocolate business, would I have done it? Probably not. If the ghost of chocolate future had shown me the pain and stress and heartache, I likely would have passed. But that did not happen. I'm happy I didn't know the future because I wouldn't have had the feeling of fulfillment and joy that has come from following this path. You're probably wondering, What kind of heartbreak could there possibly be in chocolate making? I'll tell you later!

The process of finding my personal vocation took me about five years. Upon reflection I think it might have been shorter if I'd not been so intent, intense, and in some ways desperate. But that's me and I accept that, for most of us, our greatest strengths are also our greatest weaknesses. I hope that these exercises and this chapter will help you streamline the process. If nothing else you will know that you are not alone in your struggle. A dentist wrote me recently after reading a commencement speech I gave at Mizzou. He shared his story and concluded that after a meaningful search he realized that his dentistry practice was right where he needed to be. The point is, it's possible to do this work and come right back to where you started but with renewal, purpose, and intention that was not evident before.

By the way, if you must read and just can't help yourself (I know who you are, you're me!) then I'd recommend the best book written on the subject of personal vocation: *Let Your Life Speak* by Parker Palmer. Remember, however, I am asking you to *step away from the books*, including this book! It's futile to read the next chapter and try to execute its ideas if you've not done the work I am suggesting here. This work is hard, maybe the hardest work of the entire book. It's so easy to skip over this very personal and intense emotional stuff. But it is absolutely necessary, and utterly rewarding.

EXERCISES

1. **Reflection (a step 1 exercise):** Step 1 is about making space in your life and your brain for clarity—specifically, by stopping the endless research about what you might do with your life. Have you ever experienced a moment that defined your next move, either at work or in your personal life? Get out the pen and paper and write this down. What was the pivotal moment? Where were you? Who was with you? Describe the scene and the feelings you had. Your moments will not be my moments, but they might be related in the sense that they will get you thinking.

2. **Writing "Prouds" (a step 2 exercise):** Step 2 is to find the intersection of your talents, the world's needs, and your passions. We will do this exercise a few more times in later visioning exercises throughout the book. I first heard about this from Ari Weinzweig, of Zingerman's, and have used it for years all over the world. Grab a pen and one sheet of paper and set the timer for fifteen minutes. Write a list of your "prouds"—the things

that you're proud of that you've accomplished in your life. Don't stop writing for the entire fifteen minutes. Don't restrict this list to professional accomplishments but include family, friends, hobbies, and all of it. Include characteristics you possess that you're proud of, so that your list is not only "doing" things but also "being" things.

3. **Shift Your Intention (a step 2 exercise):** Here I want to return to the prayer I repeated daily for about five years: "Dear God, please give me something else to do." The sentence is short and simple, but the depth with which I prayed this prayer is hard to describe. Beneath the words is a meditation on the heart of step 2: seeking the intersection of talent, the needs of the world, and passion. The point here is intention. You're establishing an intention to shift either what you're actually doing or your attitude about what you are currently doing. Your prayer might be: "Dear God, please renew my attitude about my business." Pick a time every day (morning is probably preferable, as opposed to right before trying to sleep) and think about these three things and what overlap there might be. While anything's possible, I don't think the answer to this question will be written in the sky. Therefore, I think it's important to ponder these questions without expecting a big answer. Socrates famously said, "There is no solution; seek it lovingly."

4. **Uncovering Your Sorrows (a step 3 exercise):** Step 3 is about looking at your sorrows in order to discover joy. This exercise does not have to take long *if* you're willing to do it. That said, you should of course take all the time you want or need. Pick up a pen and write "My great sorrow is [fill in the blank]." Repeat this again and again until you've emptied yourself of these painful memories. I am not asking for an essay, just a few words

to quickly jog your mind of the sorrow. For me it would be, "My great sorrow is my dad's death. My great sorrow is how the church people prohibited us from saying the word 'death' while my dad was sick. I felt alone." You might write, "My great sorrow is my parents' divorce." "My great sorrow is that my father abandoned our family." Perhaps you'll write, "My great sorrow is that when my father lost his job our family fell into poverty that caused suffering." The key is recalling the emotions surrounding the sorrow you've identified. Another approach, in place of or in addition to writing, would be to have this conversation with a trusted friend who is your favorite listener.

5. **Joy Meditation (a step 3 exercise):** I love to walk and maybe you can try this on a long trek in a place where your mind can wander through this idea: the other side of your sorrow and my sorrow is joy. Contemplate where you might find joy in the same emotional space as your sorrow. Do you know a place or a person who could use your service? When the idea came to me to volunteer at a local hospital I was on a walk. I also believe in prayer and I am 100 percent certain that this prayer will always be answered: "From the depths of my sorrow please reveal a place where I might serve someone who needs me." This meditation will work anywhere you can find solitude—in a room in your home, in your car, on a walk, or even on the subway with earbuds. I also think this will work as a breathing meditation. Begin with the intention that a place of service or someone who needs you will rise up to the surface of your consciousness. Take a deep breath in while saying the word "joy" and let out a long exhale while saying the word "sorrow." It's also possible that the place will come to you in conversation with a trusted friend or adviser, such as in the previous exercise.

CHAPTER 2

Develop a Business Vocation, or Else It Just Might Kill Your Business

The Real "Social Entrepreneurship"

This year, Askinosie Chocolate will have provided 1 million meals to hungry students in Tanzania and the Philippines. We're providing school lunches for 2,600 students per day. We've delivered thousands of textbooks to schools in our origin communities that previously had none and we've drilled a water well for villagers who had no potable water. Since the very beginning, we've profit shared each year with our farmer partners. We fund girls' empowerment programs in Tanzania, because when one woman rises the whole community rises with her. And we've chartered a brother program, Enlightened Boys, so the two initiatives can work in tandem to educate and empower these future leaders. At home, we involve neighborhood elementary and middle school students in many facets of our business in a program we call Chocolate University. We even take high school students with us to Tanzania for a life-changing experience. We do this all with sixteen full-time employees. And we couldn't do any of it if we didn't have a collective vocation, creating the space for us to prioritize and accomplish this work and providing the framework for success. The most formidable task, though, is bringing our hearts to it all and allowing ourselves to be transformed.

ASKINOSIE CHOCOLATE TOUCHSTONE: A PRODUCT OF CHANGE—SUSTAINABLE LUNCH PROGRAMS

We partner with schools in two of our origin communities—Kyela, Tanzania, and Davao, Philippines—to create sustainable impact and long-lasting change for their children, most of whom struggle with malnourishment. The PTAs and administrations of these schools create and/or harvest goods, in partnership with Askinosie Chocolate. In Tanzania it is a medium-grain sweet rice, and in the Philippines it is a cocoa drink called Tableya. We ship these products from the origins on the same container as our cocoa beans (no extra shipping cost), sell them in the United States, and return 100 percent of the proceeds to the school to provide meals for each of the students. In other words, these programs operate completely donation free. We provide these communities with access to market and they are empowered to feed their children.

Just as individuals can and should have a personal vocation, companies are living entities and should have a calling that gives meaning to the work of the organization. The first reason for this is survival. There's a global movement under way in which all manner of workers are seeking meaning and dignity in their work. It's a global shift in mind-set. Acknowledging, embracing, and implementing this perspective on work will mean your organization will not only survive, but thrive. Second, businesses should engage employees in work that matters. Third, a corporate calling will result in a better product or service. Companies with a vocation are better able to positively affect the lives of their employees, do good in the world, and ultimately be successful.

More than a Magazine: Vocation at Work

My friend Kim Hastreiter is the cofounder and co–editor in chief of *Paper* magazine. She and *Paper* editorial director Mickey Boardman, both fashion icons, have spent a generation living their collective vocation as a media business focused not only on the bottom line, but on the many ways they can help other people. *Paper* is an independent arts and culture publication that's been defining trends since 1984, but it's also much more than that. Kim and Mickey have both said that they could have made a lot more money over the years, but they value their independent voice more—and want to spend their time highlighting and connecting artists, designers, creators, and doers who need help, with the people who can provide it. They delight in the thrill of discovery of new talent and ideas, and sharing that with the world. Their magazine is provocative, but they use their voice to raise awareness about important issues. Kim modeled *Paper* after this ethos and even though at first she didn't realize it, it is still the driving force for the magazine to this day. "*Paper* was kind of an accident . . . but my whole mission was to take the pages and create something amazing and give these amazing artists opportunities to be discovered."[1] Their vocation? Connecting people who will benefit from knowing one another.

Kim introduced Lawren and me to many of our best customers. Because she sees value in what we do, she's made it her priority to connect us with individuals and businesses who share a similar ethos

---

1 Interview with the author, December 27, 2016.

to our company or who she knows we'd be able to collaborate with. Several years ago, she invited Lawren and me to New York to sell our chocolate in a curated food show she hosted for very small makers from across the country. One afternoon, I gave a presentation about our company and, unbeknownst to Lawren and me, Kim made sure that Target executives were there. Eventually, I was asked to present to several hundred Target executives at their headquarters; and later, our company was invited to participate in their Made to Matter program and sell our chocolate in Target stores one holiday season. Recently, Kim hosted Lawren and me in San Francisco for a tasting event for chefs. She asked her friend Liz Prueitt—of Tartine Bakery fame—to cohost so Liz could hear our story and taste our chocolate. That has also led to a meaningful partnership. Moreover, Kim and Mickey have both taken time to get to know Lawren and me personally, too. They always make us feel welcome and as though we are their honored guests.

Kim told me, "I love the combustion that happens when talented people get together. I live for it. I want to give people opportunities to be their best selves."[2] And she will go to great lengths to make things happen. Why? It's what fills her up and gives her purpose.

Kim and Mickey also intentionally allocate time and resources to their business vocation at the sacrifice of revenue. What makes this particularly striking is that they daily rub elbows with celebrities, famous folks, and the richest of the rich. Yet, Kim and Mickey haven't been motivated by outward affirmations like great financial gain. They remain true to their vocation because it's who they are as people and collectively as a business. Kim has been able to identify what is important to her and prioritize *Paper* accordingly, making thoughtful decisions throughout her thirty-plus-year career that stayed true to the vocation and vision. "I never wanted money because I knew if someone

---

2 Ibid.

gave us a lot of money then I would have to make a lot of money to pay them back. I don't want to spend my energy silo-ing everything, which is what happens in corporations," says Kim. Because *Paper* has had a clear vocation, and thus clear direction from a passionate leader, the company has evolved, grown, and thrived and continues to surpass her goals and do good for the world.

Mission Statement vs. Vocation

As the story goes, mission statements got their name in 1961 when President Kennedy challenged our country in general, and NASA in particular, to land a man on the moon within the decade. Fifty years later, I think it's safe to say the concept has become obligatory and diluted. Many mission statements are either too vague, too boring, too similar to others, or too disconnected from employees and customers. If you have a mission statement, it's likely that yours needs an overhaul. The solution? Write a vocation instead—or at least incorporate it into your mission statement. If you don't have a mission statement, then no sweat. And if you do the vocation work outlined in this book then you won't even need a mission statement. Your vocation is the calling of your organization that inspires, engages, and reminds those affected why they do what they do.

I recently asked Ari Weinzweig to describe the vocation of Zingerman's, and he pointed me to their mission statement. Their statement spells out who they are, what they do, and what they promise:

> We share the Zingerman's experience
> Selling food that makes you happy
> Giving service that makes you smile
> In passionate pursuit of our mission
> Showing love and care in all our actions
> To enrich as many lives as we possibly can.

Ours provides similar detail: "We at Askinosie Chocolate exist to craft exceptional chocolate while serving our farmers, our customers, our neighborhood, and one another, striving in all we do to leave whatever part of the world we touch better for the encounter." Those are the words that describe our vocation and they were written collectively by everyone in the company early on. The evidence of our vocation, however, is what we *do* every day. Our past actions are the measure we use to check our course, and the actions we plan for the future are our vision—our roadmap. We will take one step, then another, and another, committing to live out the words on the paper, all the while checking our route.

I am regularly asked if our vocation was part of my original business plan and the answer is yes. I knew that we would share profits with farmers before I ever made a chocolate bar. On the other hand, I could never have anticipated how our vocation would evolve over the years. In this chapter, we'll discuss how you can identify, define, integrate, and live out a vocation for your business.

THREE REASONS YOUR BUSINESS NEEDS A VOCATION

1. Survival
2. Engaged employees (including yourself!)
3. Better product or service

Why Does Your Business Need a Vocation? Survival.

In the coming century, the businesses that survive will have a vocation. And not one that was dreamed up by the marketing department as an afterthought or a campaign. The workforce of tomorrow, even more than today, will not only expect it, they will demand it.

The post–industrial revolution era is upon us. The first and second industrial revolutions, from the latter part of the eighteenth century and into the middle of the twentieth century, centered on the means and ownership of production. The focus was process and, ultimately, who owned it. There are historical markers that we can look back on over those two hundred years of big inventions and conclude that they were not simply disruptive but truly contributed to the revolution. The expectations and demands of the coming workforce are likewise giving birth to the present revolution. The factory worker of mass production a century ago didn't have time to contemplate the solutions to social injustice. The advent of artificial intelligence, virtual reality, affordable robotics, warp-speed logistics, as well as globalization and the dissemination of information, is giving rise to the worker who now has the time to say, "I want to feel fulfilled at work, to have purpose and meaning in what I do. I see this problem over here. We can, and should, do something about it." Business vocation isn't some idealistic notion; it is a direct response to the changing tides of capitalism as we know it.

The other consideration is that these technologies will de facto enhance individualism and decrease community. People are seeking a sense of belonging and community more than ever before. Therefore, organizational vocation will be paramount in the minds of employers and entrepreneurs who want to attract and retain great people. The workplace of the future might be one of the few places where we can experience community through a collective vocation that calls us to respond together in kinship with another person.

Engagement Equals Excellence

The greatest threat to our companies is stagnating disengagement among employees. The workforce wants meaningful work. A 2015 Gallup poll on American employee engagement found that only one in three workers are "engaged in their work," defined as those who are "involved in, enthusiastic about, and committed to their work and workplace."[3] That has remained unchanged for the fifteen-plus years that Gallup has been measuring engagement. Comparatively, a 2013 Gallup poll found that the number is even lower worldwide, at only 13 percent.[4] This is unacceptable and avoidable. It puts our mental, physical, emotional, and spiritual health in jeopardy. Moreover, it puts the health of companies and our economy at risk. The responsibility rests on our own shoulders to take control of our work life, to take action to create meaning and infuse it into our businesses, teams, and work groups. If we can implement our business vocation then we can offer other entrepreneurs a sign that things can be different and better. Involved, enthusiastic, and committed employees are engaged workers. They are fulfilled.

The psychologist Abraham Maslow's theory of the hierarchy of needs tells us what we need to do at work to have engaged workers. We strive to meet the physiological needs of our team at work. What does that look like? One very simple example is that we take time to stretch every day. We also have a quarterly lunch together as a group, which the company pays for. We also take field trips. Once a quarter, we take half a day off of work and go see a baseball game, play miniature golf, go bowling, anything fun that's outside of work. We've also worked hard to ensure that all of our employees are at living wage or above; all of the togetherness in the world won't pay the utility bill.

We want our employees to feel safe in their jobs. We report the finances of the company in a huddle every Tuesday so that everyone is on the same page with where we are in relation to our goals and our

---

3 http://www.gallup.com/poll/181289/majority-employees-not-engaged-despite -gains-2014.aspx.

4 http://www.gallup.com/poll/165269/worldwide-employees-engaged-work.aspx, a survey of employees in 141 countries.

company's overall financial health. There's an understanding among us that we're rowing the boat in the same direction. We rarely make big financial decisions without consulting the entire group. Most importantly, we share the successes with employees by giving them a stake in the outcome. This, maybe more than anything else, lends a sense of security to all of us that we are in it together working toward the same goals.

We want our employees to feel a sense of belonging, that they are connected to something larger than themselves. Our work with nearby schools, working directly with farmers, and even receiving praise, recognition, and awards for our chocolate, are a few of the things that give all of us a sense of belonging to each other and something bigger.

Self-esteem is crucial to engagement. We work to cultivate a culture of respect and appreciation among our team by prioritizing diversity and dedicating ourselves to making sure our coworkers feel accepted and respected by each other. We provide a workplace where public praise is common. People know of their contribution and where it fits in our vocation.

Recently, the spouse of one of our employees was diagnosed with a life-threatening illness. We are doing everything we can to help, including allowing flexible hours and time off during treatments, checking in, and simply listening. Our team is also taking turns to provide dinner once a week for the family. The message it sends is loud and clear: we all care about you and your suffering.

If we can invest in these human needs, then we have the chance to serve our employees and bring hope to everyone in the organization for a more fulfilled life.

Employee engagement includes you, too, by the way! Owners, founders, CEOs, entrepreneurs—you need to feel energized, to be mentally and physically focused, and to lead by example. This is necessary for a deeper reason: self-preservation and the chance to become your "true self," as Thomas Merton would say.

Bad Attitude, Bad Product or Service

Vocations provide meaning and purpose. Products or services created with intention, by people who feel they're contributing toward a higher purpose, will undoubtedly be higher quality. This is true for both you and your employees. Kahlil Gibran said, "For if you bake bread with indifference, you bake a bitter bread that feeds but half man's hunger." The same is true for chocolate!

Of course it's true that workers within an organization that doesn't have a vocation can still feel they're a part of something bigger and greater. But if my business has a defined vocation, the impact is palpable. We all know what our vocation is and we're working together toward a common goal. There's a fulfillment in this, which creates a focus and concentration on each individual job as part of the bigger picture. How could this not create a better product, and thus a better experience for not just ourselves but our customers?

Making the best chocolate we can is part of our vocation and I think our end result speaks for itself. Serving our neighborhood is also part of our vocation. Different people at the factory focus on different parts of our vocation, which is efficient, and helps define our roles. And because of all the communication and support baked into our business model and our daily processes, we're all still functioning together as one unit toward our vocation in its entirety.

Business vocations also improve efficiency in other ways. Ours helps us make decisions. We use our vocation to minimize distraction and thus, we're more productive. This means higher quality and service because we don't need to waste time pondering certain opportunities that we know don't fit our vocation and our vision for the company.

Every week, five of our team members gather together to taste a random sampling of a couple of our products. We are intense and methodical. During one tasting a few years ago we started noticing a flavor defect with one particular chocolate bar. We tasted this bar repeatedly on multiple occasions and analyzed the possible sources of the problem. Our eventual conclusion was that it was the cocoa beans themselves. I told Lawren, who agreed with our assessment, that we should stop selling that bar. This meant we would be forgoing thousands of dollars in revenue. We'd never done anything like this before, and we haven't had to since. But we reminded ourselves of our vocation, which is serving our farmers *and* making great, high-quality chocolate. This was a case of quality winning over everything else: our own profitability; the fact that some might not notice that we had a less-than-perfect chocolate bar on the market; and farmers who might be upset with us. It was painful, but it was the right choice. Since we practice direct trade with the farmers and have a long relationship with them, we were able to have honest discussions with them about the harvesting practice that led to the issue with the off-flavor beans. It was a learning experience for all, adjustments were made, and the beans have been excellent ever since.

Employees First: Appreciation and Kinship

Meaningful work is both internal and external. It's internal in that I have a sense of personal dignity during the workday because of *who* I am, not *what* I do. This is a daily practice, not an event. Meaningful work is external, though, in that I hope to let the light of my dignity be a lamp for my fellow workers and shine collectively upon the work we decide to do together for good purposes.

Whether you call it culture, environment, foundation, servant leadership, or, more formally, "core values," it begins with how you make your employees feel. We must get a handle on the space where people spend eight hours a day. In this space they breathe, work, talk, think, create, interact, laugh, hope, dream, eat, drink. Our hearts are here, so let's stop pretending we need to leave them out of business. Of course our employees possess dignity outside of or apart from their work, but why wouldn't we aim to cultivate an environment where they feel those same values about their job? We must do everything we can in all humility to prepare and take care of our workplace culture as if it is a treasure.

One of the precepts of our vocation is service to each other within the company. There's something we do at the chocolate factory to show our appreciation for our employees that is simple, no cost, and one of the most touching things I've seen. In addition to birthdays, we celebrate what we call "work-iversaries." When it's someone's work-iversary, we take time at the conclusion of our Tuesday huddle and recognize that person with a favorite food or drink. Most importantly, though, everyone forms a semicircle around the celebrated person and one by one we tell that individual what we love, admire, respect, or appreciate about him or her. The person says nothing, just takes it all in. Sometimes there are tears—the good kind.

A few months ago Kat, our sales director, had her work-iversary with us. She was perched on a stool, and our entire team gathered our chairs around her. One by one, each of her coworkers shared what they love about her. Lawren started off and said, "What I appreciate about you, Kat, is your unparalleled dedication and loyalty—that I can truly rely on you as my right hand." I said, "Kat, what I admire about you is that you never give up, you are never discouraged, and even when things seem tough you always have a positive attitude." I remember Megan saying, "What I love about you, Kat, is that you exude excellence in everything you do; not just in work but in every aspect of life." Just as Megan was looking right at Kat, speaking these words, from the heart, Kat's eyes filled up and spilled over and down her cheeks. After everyone spoke, we presented Kat with a card and we enjoyed macarons, one of her favorite snacks. After a meeting like this concludes, everyone goes back to their job and the task at hand, but the mood is lighter and the energy is electric. It's still surprising to me after years of doing this how difficult—and also how encouraging, uplifting, and affirming—it is to listen to someone saying something like this directly to you, looking at you, and meaning it. It's so simple. But it's a powerful expression of dignity for the person praising and the person receiving, as well as the entire group! It's an example of the kinship within our team.

"Kinship" is a very important word at our company. I borrowed it from Jesuit priest Father Greg Boyle, who introduced me to the concept of kinship in his book *Tattoos on the Heart*, in which he talks about his work with Los Angeles gangs over the past thirty years. Kinship is such an important concept to us that we hired a chief kinship officer, Missy. It's her job to integrate this notion into the reality of our day-to-day work.

Not long ago, our facilities manager and chocolate maker, Kevin, wrote me a letter:

> It has been an honor to work here [and] I'm filled with a great sense of pride about what I am able to contribute. So . . . if the ship were to go down tomorrow I want you to know it would have been worth it. You made a difference not only in the lives of customers, communities across the globe, but in mine as well. I have learned things here about discipline and commitment that will be passed on to my children and held close to my heart forever. I admire the sense of urgency with which you strive to inaugurate God's present and coming Kingdom here on Earth.

His attitude is what I had hoped and planned for, for me and my team, when I founded this company. This is the pinnacle of success for me and he's right; if "the ship were to go down tomorrow" it would have been worth it. I don't save many things, but I've put that letter in a safe place because his sentiment is a treasure to me.

It's Up to You for Employees to See Themselves as Part of the Bigger Picture

Walking along, a person encountered a stonemason and asked what he was doing. The mason replied, "I am working on these heavy rocks, carrying and chiseling them all day long so I can get paid." Walking further, the person asked another mason what he was doing and that mason replied, "I'm a stonemason, building a great cathedral to the glory of God in which people will come to worship for centuries in the future." The difference between the cathedral builder and a stonemason? Attitude, even though they have the same "job." There's a similar anecdote about President John F. Kennedy. In 1962 he visited NASA headquarters for the first time. While touring the facility, he introduced himself to a janitor who was mopping the floor and asked him what he did at NASA. The janitor replied, "I'm helping put a man on the moon!" He's a cathedral builder! He must have exuded dignity and very clearly believed in the NASA vocation of something much bigger than launching a rocket into outer space.

In order to create an environment in which people have the best chance of believing that their work is significant, we must believe it to be true. Every person has the basic human right to believe and know the work that they do matters. Martin Luther King Jr. said it best: "If a man is called to be a street sweeper, he should sweep streets even as Michelangelo painted, or Beethoven composed music, or Shakespeare wrote poetry. He should sweep streets so well that all the hosts of heaven and earth will pause to say, 'Here lived a great street sweeper who did his job well.' No work is insignificant. All labor that uplifts humanity has dignity and importance and should be undertaken with painstaking excellence." It would be easy for our four-person packaging team to feel their tasks were menial. But our packaging is recognized and awarded because each of them care deeply about executing every small piece with excellence, and they know that their work contributes to the growth of our company, and money in the hands of farmers.

Our job as business leaders is to set the stage for success every day. What are the things we can do in our organizations to make it more likely that our team members see themselves as "helping put a man on the moon"? Here's the great news: Your company ethos is not defined by the thing that you make. The sum of your business is greater than the parts. The collective work of your group is bigger and more significant than one person or the service you provide. If Jack Stack can lead the way in open-book management and teach a generation of entrepreneurs about company ethos while remanufacturing heavy equipment transmissions, then what we "make" or "do" will not hold us back as we lay the foundation for dignity at work.

How to Build a Culture of Dignity—
the Foundation for Business Vocation

HOW TO BUILD A CULTURE OF DIGNITY

1. Value your team.
2. Model dignity and service.
3. Integrate these abstract notions into concrete business practices, but start with employees first.
4. Maintain the culture.

Create an environment where people believe that they are valued. Of course it should go without saying that a good leader truly does value his or her employees. Modeling this behavior yourself gives the best chance that your team will follow. If I'm not approaching my work with a dignified attitude, then I'm setting my employees up for failure. If I'm not walking around thinking I'm sending a man or woman to the moon, then why would anyone else? If a sense of dignity isn't palpable in your workplace, check yourself first. One helpful thing to keep in mind: internal dignity is often manifested by outward joy. Do our colleagues see us as joyful? Do we take time to talk to our coworkers about their lives? I am by no means perfect at this and there are many days when I fail to measure up to my own standard. But on the days I'm not feeling it, I aim to fake it. I learned this as a teenager from reading Dale Carnegie, who said, "Act enthusiastic and you'll be enthusiastic."

Another way to establish this foundation is by inspiring your team. Are you aiming to serve your employees? Are you kind to vendors, customers, and even yourself? Our team should not perceive us as heroes up on pedestals, but as people in whom they can see themselves. They see the possibilities because you show them the way. The example you set—how you lead—when things are tough is just as important as it is when things are great.

Take concrete steps to integrate these notions into your everyday business practices. This means there should be activities on the calendar that exercise the dignity muscle of everyone in the group. Take whatever notion you have of "employee appreciation" and push it a step further. Depending on the size of your business, this challenge may be greater. Remember that this is top down. For example, we have a chief operating officer and someone who integrates kinship at our little company, but that doesn't relieve me of my duty to let everyone who works here know that I care about them. I can do that directly by simply having conversations with each of them and indirectly by the things we do as a company.

Another indirect way to build this foundation for vocation is to recognize your employees, their life events, their families—celebrate their joys and share in their sorrows. It doesn't even need to cost money. Try simple affirmations of gratitude for a job well done. Or just saying "thank you." Voltaire said, "Appreciation is a wonderful thing. It makes what is excellent in others belong to us as well." Ultimately, you can celebrate all of the birthdays you want but if your employees think deep down that you don't care about them and appreciate their work, then the cake and cookies are simply window dressing.

Once we have a grasp of this foundation, once we're living it and seeing proof of it, then we can make room for a collective vocation. This is the place in which people are working to "send a woman to the moon," even if they're rebuilding bulldozer transmissions.

Before the organization can begin finding its collective vocation, the culture of dignity, appreciation, kindness, and community should be established. However, if you wait until the climate is perfect then you'll never move on to the next phase. During our Chocolate University trip to Tanzania in 2014, the young men we brought with us met with a group of young men at one of the schools we work with. The women were on the other side of the school, participating in a graduation ceremony for the Empowered Girls program we operate. The boys' discussion was free ranging, with lots of questions from their boys to ours. The local boys let loose with their opinions and I primarily listened.

I left that meeting dreaming about a boys' program for the school, too. It was obvious to me that if the girls' program was ever going to be truly successful, the boys needed empowerment education also. This fact is also obvious to experts working on gender equality in developing countries, and yet when we began seeking information about such initiatives we quickly found there was none. Virtually no one was operating a program like this for boys. There wasn't even really any curriculum. I asked former State Department and United Nations girls' empowerment experts if they could suggest a boys' program template for us to adapt in rural Tanzania. Nothing. Discouraged, we felt like perhaps we'd reached the end of the road. Not to mention, we didn't exactly feel qualified to create a curriculum. We're chocolate makers, not international development experts. Then we asked ourselves: Does this fit within our vocation framework? Do we feel strongly about it? We decided to go for it and we held our first Enlightened Boys meeting in August 2016. Is it perfect? No. Is it helping to make a difference? Yes. The boys are meeting with Saraphiner, our field representative, and a faculty sponsor every Wednesday. We're already seeing the benefits as the boys are more motivated to attend school. Most importantly, they want to learn more.

ASKINOSIE CHOCOLATE TOUCHSTONE: EMPOWERED GIRLS AND ENLIGHTENED BOYS

Empowered Girls is a grassroots organization founded by our friend Kellen Msseemmaa. Kellen, a native of Uganda, operates programs for young women in schools throughout East Africa. In 2010, we worked with her to charter a club at Mwaya Secondary School and now we operate a second club at Mababu Primary School in Tanzania as well. The goal of the program is to empower young women to be strong, confident, successful leaders by educating them on topics including gender equality, sexual and reproductive health, cultural norms, and even skills training. We've since founded a brother program, Enlightened Boys, to complement the education and training for the young women. They work in tandem to encourage a more egalitarian community.

Three Paths to Business Vocation

There are three possible paths by which your business vocation could be transmitted throughout the company. One way is that you start a company based on your personal vocation. This is what happened with me and it's the path of many entrepreneurs. Another is that, once a company is under way, the CEO/founder/leader begins some vocational work, involves the leadership team, and inspires others in the company to join them. Or sometimes the seed for a group vocation comes from a small team of employees who inspire colleagues to join the cause and ultimately the leadership of the business joins in. Of course there are many variations on this theme and other combinations are possible. Before executing the steps below you need to decide who is participating in this process. Is it your leadership team, everyone in the company, your family, or just you? In my case it was me alone because there were no other employees when I started putting it all together.

The Evolution—Action and When Others Join In

The most important part of your business vocation? Living it out. It's critical for your organization to actively seek out opportunities to put the vocation into practice, every day. In order for the vocation to be truly transformational, it must be woven into the fabric of your organizational culture, with a priority on action. Ideas are great, but a vocation isn't effective as a change agent if it isn't integrated into the business, top down and bottom up. This might manifest itself in a few ways. Perhaps job titles change slightly, or your approach to how you reward employees changes, or you find yourself shuffling duties and tasks because priorities have shifted. Not everyone within your organization will actively participate in the business vocation and that's okay. For now, it's important to understand that a business vocation isn't a business vocation if it isn't making waves within your organization.

Get ready for others in the organization to bring new ideas and dreams. When team members actively contribute to the business vocation by proposing some of their own ideas, this is the best part! It's a joy for me when others within Askinosie Chocolate begin new great initiatives that I had nothing to do with. For example, it was not my idea to start a summer school program at our factory. It was our chief kinship officer Missy's idea. It was not my idea to start a program of providing feminine hygiene products to girls in the Tanzanian village where we buy beans; that came from Lawren.

The process to uncovering your business vocation is very similar to the steps in chapter 1 for uncovering your personal vocation. The big difference is that we'll adjust some main ideas to fit a group of people working together within an organization.

STEPS TO UNCOVER YOUR BUSINESS VOCATION

Step 1:   Don't try to find it by endless research.
Step 2:   Inventory your company's talents and passions, look at what the world needs, and host a vocation summit.
Step 3:   Begin with delicately looking at the sorrows of your leadership team.
Step 4:   Start doing something.
Step 5:   Open your hearts to a need, with no expectation of profit or benefit.

Step 1: Don't Try to Find It by Endless Research

You want to identify your business vocation? You will not find it in a book or online. Not even in this book! Why? Because it's personal. It's based on you—the entrepreneur, founder, leader—and your unique vocation. The most efficient path toward this goal is to simply move to step 2. You will not find the answer to the question "How can my business make an impact in the world?" in the Google search box. I wish it was that easy. But the work ahead of you in these next steps is so much more rewarding. We need to answer this question organically, from the heart, and it will be offline for the most part. Plus, despite our desire to the contrary, there is no formula for this. It is primarily a matter of the heart and not the head. Following the guidelines here will require work, group introspection, and an open heart.

Step 2: Inventory Your Company's Talents and Passions, Look at What the World Needs, and Host a Vocation Summit

We'll start with something easy: what does your company make or do? And now: what do you make or do *best*? What are the greatest talents of your leadership team or employees?

Now on the flip side: what are some needs of your community? Sometimes it's easiest—and even best—to focus on your neighborhood alone. What can your company do to solve some of those problems? No solution is too small.

Vocation is often thought of as religious, since its common use is related to a "calling" into the priesthood. Author, thinker, and educator Parker Palmer has written extensively on this topic and articulated a different view from the common perception that vocation equals God's calling on our lives. In *Let Your Voice Speak*, he says:

> Our deepest calling is to grow into our own authentic selfhood, whether or not it conforms to some image of who we ought to be. As we do so, we will not only find the joy that every human being seeks—we will also find our path of authentic service in the world. True vocation joins self and service, as Frederick Buechner asserts when he defines vocation as "the place where your deep gladness meets the world's deep need."

Can a business have an "authentic selfhood"? Yes! It can and should. I think Askinosie Chocolate does. Can you think of companies large or small that have an "authentic selfhood"? *Paper* magazine is one example. Patagonia is another. Its mission statement is: "Build the best product, cause no unnecessary harm, use business to inspire and implement solutions to the environmental crisis." The company has been realizing this mission for nearly fifty years. It began with founder Yvon Chouinard finding the intersection of his deep gladness and the world's deep need. Patagonia has been at the forefront of environmental activism since the 1980s. The company's leaders have told their story well over the ensuing decades. You could plumb the depths of the second half of their mission statement for a long time and barely scratch the surface. One of the most interesting benefits they offer as a company is their employee environmental internship program, in which they give an employee full pay for two months, while on leave of absence, to volunteer for an environmental nonprofit. Clearly, their mission statement embodies their vocation. This project is the evidence of a vocation activity at the company that gives life to the words.

It's important to note here that no company is perfect. There is no magical formula by which you can achieve pure, flawless execution of your vocation. But that shouldn't paralyze you from action, from pushing onward, from moving the needle forward ever so slightly and with a few mistakes along the way. The aim is to be authentic to *your* business vocation, and also to be transparent and truthful. Our vocation is about prioritizing relationships, chocolate, and service. We make every effort to live these values out in the various initiatives described in this book. But there's also a million things we can do better— our packing and shipping materials, for example. We use Styrofoam to protect our chocolate and keep it cool. Styrofoam is admittedly bad for the environment. It's important to us to continue seeking alternatives, but we have other priorities related to kinship that will take precedence, because empowering our employees, neighborhood, and origin communities is written in our vocation and using Styrofoam is not. Again, that's not to say the environment isn't important to us. But honesty and dedication to your vocation is key when considering priorities. It all goes back to the promises you make to your customers. If you promise it, then you're holding your company to a higher standard as it relates to the promise. Patagonia, for example, promises commitment to the environment and therefore holds itself to a higher standard. Your business can do anything, but not everything.

Host a Vocation Summit

Feeling stuck or overwhelmed? Try hosting a vocation summit at your business. This may be the single most effective method to establish your business vocation and for that reason I've broken it down into smaller exercises. Maybe you're the only one attending, or perhaps it's your leadership team. You will have some homework and you will need to assign tasks to others in the group. This summit will take place over two or three meetings. Here's what a vocation summit looks like:

1. **List your company's "prouds."** Take fifteen minutes and review your company's core skill set. Make a list and write it down in a lightning round with your team. Remember the writing exercise in chapter 1 listing your "prouds"? You will need to do it again, but this time you are making a list of the things your company is great at. It's important to reduce this list to details, details, and more details. Maybe you're a plastic surgeon and great at face-lifts. For example, if I were making this list today for my company I might list that we are really good at managing and forecasting cash flow, or that we're great at enacting change with our farmer partners in Tanzania.

2. **List your company's acts of service.** Take another fifteen minutes and write down what your company is already doing to serve people. This could be serving each other or those in your neighborhood, your community, or somewhere along

your supply chain. Include in this list the major charitable contributions your company makes. Then take a few more minutes and discuss *why* you give. Is it for marketing purposes? That's fine, but call it what it is. Or is it for some other charitable purpose for which your company has not and will not receive recognition? What motivated that decision? Write it down. Include individual service projects that people at your business are working on that they are passionate about. These are not necessarily related to the business, but they are up for discussion because your leaders obviously care about them.

For example, we've had a middle school program for many years in which we connect with students at our neighborhood school throughout the year as part of our Chocolate University project. This is part of our vocation. Recently the faculty sponsor, Julia, approached us about partnering with the school district to host a middle school summer school program. One vocation idea leads to another, right? Well, it's not that easy. When our chief kinship officer brought this idea to our weekly leadership huddle, it felt too big and I asked her to table it. She brought it up again at the following meeting. I was feeling pressure to green-light a program that I thought sounded too big for us to execute well. I expressed concern over our capability to host a summer school and take students to Tanzania in the same summer, saying, "We've got to remember that we have a business to run: making and selling chocolate." Missy was passionate about this project, though, and succinctly explained how the idea fits with our vocation, how little time it would take to prepare, and the possible impact it would have on students. And then she quickly added the magic words: "I will head this up and you won't have to do anything unless as we get closer to summer you want to teach a couple of the lessons and interact with the kids."

Fast-forward eight months and she was not only right, but I loved the kids and it was one of the most successful things we've done. We are planning to do it again this summer. That decision involved figuring out how to balance and allocate our time and money. Our business supports our vocation and our vocation supports our business at the same time. They are interdependent. In this case, that means the summer school program makes us a better company, and yet we need at least modest financial health to tackle projects like this.

You may be asking: but what about "mission creep"? That is a very important thing to watch for! But it's more important for the actual company mission than the business vocation; and it can be managed. I would much rather be faced with this problem than a dead mission that exists as words in a frame on the wall for people to see but not live out.

3. **Identify who you can support in your business.** Before convening the next meeting of your vocation summit to discuss this topic, there will be some premeeting brainstorming homework. Who do you touch in your industry that might need your company for some reason? Are there any vulnerable people in your supply chain? Do you source garments in Bangladesh? Do you import furniture from Malaysia? Do you sell maritime insurance to companies that export from vulnerable farmers? Do you own a coffee shop? Do you buy from local farmers for your restaurant? You know where we are going with this list. Here is the essence of the process: where can you plug in and support, partner, befriend, and deepen relationships with a sense of mutuality of service? We're answering the question "What does the world need?" and we're defining "world" within the context of your industry. Bring this list with you to the vocation summit and spend fifteen minutes discussing all of these possibilities.

Come ready to discuss other people and groups you have not considered.

Cocoa is the main ingredient in our supply chain. We trade directly with cocoa farmers around the world. That means I travel to each origin country every year to meet with farmers, check on that year's crop, maintain relationships, open our books to the farmers, profit share with them, and taste chocolate made from their beans. This is central to our business vocation because our farmer partners are critical to our product and also are in varying degrees of poverty. We asked ourselves on day one: how can we be the most involved and connected with farmers? What does this look like in practice? Our relationship with our farmers best represents what I mean by "mutuality." Yes, the farmers are what we might call "poor," but we don't stand over here as the buyer and they don't stand over there as the seller with us providing services *to* them. We are colleagues working together toward a common goal. We are friends. And in that role we learn from them much more than they could ever learn from us. They teach us about hospitality, community, and joy. In the midst of the relationship, we discuss ways we can partner with them to assist on projects where we're suited to help. That is what it means for our company's collective skills to meet the needs of the world.

One thing we've become good at is helping people write their own "vision of greatness." I've assisted churches, students, businesses, and farmer groups. Our Tanzania farmer partners are in their third year of a ten-year vision plan that we helped facilitate. One of the facets of their vision is to have a wood-working business in order to diversify, so they are not totally dependent on cocoa. Another point in their vision was to have an office where they could meet and work on their cooperative business. This year, that office was built; it was financed by them and three years ago it was merely a dream. We've been there with them for the planning every step of the way—not in the details, but to encourage and lend guidance and support when they asked. During our second visioning meeting with the farmers we met in a vacant classroom at Mababu Primary School. Our Chocolate University students from Missouri were with us, and the co-op leader, Mamma Mpoki, was sitting in the front row next to Lawren. As is typical with the visioning process, we asked the farmers to speak as though they were ten years into the future. The farmers took turns standing to share their dreams. Mr. Franklin, one of the most active farmers in the co-op, stood up and said, "It's August 7, 2023. I woke up this morning and my bed was a mattress; I looked up and we had a ceiling in the house; my wife went to the market in our car and bought the food we need." As he sat back down, tears were running down his face. He had never let himself dream into the future like this before and was moved by the experience. We were accustomed to his wide smile and encompassing hand-shake; we hadn't seen him cry before. I was at the front of the room leading this discussion and it was hard to keep it together. Another farmer stood up, an elder in the village, a warm and confident leader named Mr. Livingston. He said the discussion made him feel like a young man again.

4. **Identify who you can support in your community.** For the vocation summit's next discussion of meeting the world's needs, define "world" as the neighborhood where your physical spaces (factory, office, distribution center—anything) reside. What is the need you see on your street? You can survey groups in your community to discover the real needs of people and groups close to you. Are there schools in your neighborhood that might need the skills of your business? Does your company do something

that students would enjoy learning more about? You can probably tell that I am very biased in favor of starting programs to help students. I would like to know a school that wouldn't benefit from help. Do you make ice cream? What students wouldn't like to learn about that? Spend fifteen minutes talking about your neighborhood. Again, you will need to do some homework to prepare for this discussion. If you want to quickly learn about the needs of your city I suggest making an appointment with someone at your local community foundation. These are a little-known repository of information about local health, education, housing, nutrition, and nonprofit needs.

Our factory neighborhood is legally "blighted." It's in the process of being revitalized, but still, there is pervasive poverty in the blocks around us. The largest homeless shelter in our town was a little less than one hundred yards away from our front door and there were about eighty kids, on average, staying there every night. Those children went to the schools in our neighborhood.

We started Chocolate University the same month we sold our first chocolate bar, because it was important to us to engage the kids of the neighborhood in our business. We wanted to inspire them about small business as a force for good and expose them to a world beyond Springfield, Missouri. We wanted to welcome them into our little chocolate factory and show them love and hospitality, and share chocolate together. We began the program at Boyd Elementary nearly a decade ago and it's still going strong. It's a back-and-forth relationship; we are involved in curriculum units and either the kids visit our factory for hands-on learning or we are in the classroom. Various folks from our company, from production to sales, volunteer to participate in these sessions. We make sure that our partnership with the school is not extra work for the teachers, but an adjunct that works for them and is fun for their students. We love spending time in the classrooms. By the end of the year, the students feel like they are part of our business. About nine years ago, we chartered the Pipkin Middle School program, and then by 2009 we were brainstorming the high school bean-to-bar immersion program, all of which continues to this day.

The list above may look like a lot, but anyone can do it. We don't have a philanthropy department at Askinosie Chocolate and that's part of what makes this work in schools, villages, farms, and our neighborhood so natural. It all fits together in our daily activities at work.

And yet, sometimes we fall short; sometimes this work brings heartache. A few years ago we were selecting our new class of Chocolate University high school students. There were about eighty students vying for fourteen positions. At the start of the program, one of our students got into serious trouble at school and we had to remove the student from Chocolate University. It wasn't easy to call this student and the parents to let them know of our decision, but we approach things like this as we do any other business decision. One time a mother of two of our students called to complain that "too many adults" were going on the trip, saying, "I thought this was for the kids." At first, I was angry and aggravated and wanted to respond with, "Really? I am taking your kids on a trip of a lifetime and you're complaining that we're being too safe?" Instead, I stayed calm, tried to recognize that something else might be at play, and explained that I needed adults to help me supervise the trip and that this was, at its heart, a business trip. Her reactions made it clear to me that it would be best if her teenagers were not part of the trip. I was sad it had come to this, but we ended up selecting the next students on the list.

We succeed and fail at the service part of our vocation, just like we succeed and fail at the making-great-chocolate part of our vocation.

5. **Keep your mind on your mission and your mission on your mind.** Don't think that just because I've got you thinking about vulnerable people your vocation must be about people in poverty. Remember the cathedral builder? He was not part of a company with a stated vocation. However, I can see the construction overseer of Notre Dame in the year eleven-hundred-something encouraging his group of stonemasons daily that they were making history and crafting something that would remain standing for centuries as a symbol of God on earth. The mission to the moon was not only about sending a man to the moon, it was about America. It was the active expression of patriotism, winning the cold war, and exploration of the final frontier. These ideals eclipse one person or one company, in that the mission alone is too big to fail. Does your company have such a mission? Maybe you have a mission that's too big to fail and you don't know it. Possibly, it's the position from which you are observing that obstructs your view.

6. **Find the intersections.** Try graphing your conversations from these meetings. Do any of these ideas meet anywhere? If you were to draw a Venn diagram, what overlaps? You can plot this in a spreadsheet with topics down the left side and names of participants at the top, with Xs in the cells that cover the topic. I recommend drawing these conclusions in a separate vocation meeting, to allow a few days for the earlier discussions to soak in.

Step 3: Begin with Delicately Looking at the Sorrows of Your Leadership Team

One of my favorite authors, Joseph Campbell, says we are called to "participate joyfully in the sorrows of the world." Your leadership team will participate as a group in the exercise of uncovering sorrows. Collectively, you will work together toward the ultimate goal of finding common joys that will become your business's vocation. This work is difficult in a group setting but ultimately endlessly rewarding. However, it must be approached with a manner of thoughtfulness, compassion, and empathy.

First, assign some homework to your team. Ask them to try the Uncovering Your Sorrows writing exercise from chapter 1 at home, away from work, on their own. Your vocation team should come to the meeting prepared and hopefully willing to share some sorrows in their life. To begin discussion, ask each person in the group to write down a few words about the sorrow they've experienced—and don't include their name. You can collect these and read these sentences aloud to the group. There is no discussion at this point, only reading and listening. Then go back and read them again, but this time ask the group if they can think of a joy that might be on the other side of the sorrow listed. If someone writes, "My brother was born with special needs and other kids made fun of him at school," then you would ask the group what joys could rise up from that pain. For example, if that sorrow resonated with others in the group, then what joy is possible in working with a nearby school for children with special needs? What about employment opportunities at your company for people with special needs? The pain and sorrow can be replaced with joy.

Second, ask your group to review the insights from step 2 above (which will be in writing, and which you should make available during this session). The group will review the intersections of company talents, passions, and needs of the world. Where is the crossover? For example, you own a CPA firm, you've identified that your company is super passionate about helping really small businesses understand how better accounting can make a difference in their bottom line, and from this exercise you realize the obvious: that your offices are in an impoverished neighborhood. Is there a connection to any sorrows from your team? Can you draw a line from the work you're doing now and any of those sorrows? Maybe not, and that is okay. At a minimum, if people listen during this time then the real breakthrough will be the discovery of possible vocations not previously considered. In the CPA firm example, let's say that our founder grew up in poverty. It was painful for her. During this exercise she and others in leadership discuss the connections between what they are good at, who might need them, and the joy that might come from the pain that connects the whole story. This CPA firm comes up with the idea to engage a limited number of families in their neighborhood in some new financial literacy classes they plan to teach.

This meeting of sorrows and joys should be separate from the other vocation meetings listed above. The point here is that you're looking for common ground, for things that resonate with the group. Opening up about personal joys and sorrows could uncover themes.

Set ground rules in advance of your meeting. For example, anyone can pass on discussion at any time. Don't require everyone to talk. Ask people to practice deep listening during this meeting.

In a roundabout way, our work with schools and students stems from a sorrow-to-joy story in my past. I had so many positive school experiences growing up in my town. The standout is Mr. Paul Elmore, who was my sixth grade teacher during the time my dad was very sick with cancer. He saved me during that time; his class was so much fun, it was a distraction. He was a young man, with a newly minted teaching certificate, who looked like John Denver. More importantly, he asked about how things were going at home, when others wouldn't. I innately sensed Mr. Elmore's empathy, even before he told me that his own mother had recently died. He knew how difficult things were at my house and he knew my dad, because he was the president of the Hickory Hills PTA. He told me how much he respected my father: "Shawn, your dad is a fighter and I know you're going to be just like him." He wrote notes on my homework papers like, "Shawn—I can see you're going to be a lawyer someday just like your dad. Keep up the good work." For all I know that could have been the same day that I found my dad lying in the driveway, having fallen after a chemo treatment, in his own vomit. There were many sad days like that. When Mr. Elmore praised my father it made me feel good; it gave me hope for the next day. His simple kindness allowed me to breathe.

I feel a deep sense of duty to be to students what Mr. Elmore was to me and we've infused this notion throughout our Chocolate University project.

Step 4: Start Doing Something

I often hear praise for what we're doing at our company, immediately followed by, "We'll hopefully be able to do this kind of work when we have more [fill in the blank: capital, employees, experience, time, partners, etc.]." My advice to you: don't wait. Start doing something now. I promise you can, no matter what condition your organization is in. Once your vocation team has met as I've outlined here, then draft a vocation vision of greatness with your group—and begin the work. At the end of the chapter, I will explain how you can write this vision of greatness based on what Ari Weinzweig and his books have taught us.

One of the keys to a successful vocation is to begin. Roll up your sleeves and start. It won't be easy, but don't get weighed down with the what and the how. I'll also reiterate: serving on a board is not your business vocation. It is essential that you go, do, connect, struggle, and even suffer. Jean Vanier, Catholic theologian, author, and founder of L'Arche, the international federation dedicated to the creation and growth of homes, programs, and support networks for people who have intellectual disabilities, reminds us that we need not have lofty goals:

"But let us not put our sights too high. We do not have to be saviors of the world! We are simply human beings, enfolded in weakness and in hope, called together to change our world one heart at a time." One heart at a time. And it starts with you (and me).

We've funded many projects by giving tours of our chocolate factory over the past decade. We've never kept that money for ourselves; instead we've set it aside in a separate Chocolate University account at our local community foundation. Several years ago we discovered that the kids at the nearby homeless shelter didn't have a place to do homework, so we took money from that account and renovated a room in the basement of the shelter. We bought computers and turned it into a study room for the kids to work with their parents on homework and hopefully have some sense of normalcy. We've also raised thousands of dollars in our community foundation fund from customers and friends across the country in order to afford to take our Chocolate University students to Tanzania.

It's easy to be tempted by all of the ways in which your business can serve the community. These causes may be legitimate, but they can also be distractions. The key is to select your projects based on your vocation. Does it fit within your vocation framework? If not, then it's something you should thoughtfully pass on. You can't do it all, nor should you try. The idea is depth versus breadth. However, there may very well be several areas of community engagement within your vocation, just like we find at Askinosie Chocolate. Before your company begins a new initiative, it's imperative to ask if it makes sense and if you can execute it with excellence.

It seems like we do a lot, and we do, but for every initiative we start there are ten more that we've passed on. For example, we've received requests from two schools we work with in Tanzania to build dormitories, one for students and the other for teachers. Generally speaking, school dormitories in developing countries are a positive thing. However, after thought and consideration we remain unchanged in our opinion that it's not something we can take on. It's critical that our projects are consistent with our direct trade practices. Erecting school buildings involves the government and we aim to work with as few regulatory layers as possible because we've found it's the best way to do the most good, especially in association with our farmer partners. Additionally, nutrition in schools has always been a primary focus, first and foremost. It's important to us that we get those programs sustainable and functioning extremely well before we move to another project.

Step 5: Open Your Hearts to a Need, with No Expectation of Profit or Benefit

I don't think I would be writing this book but for the fact that I continue with this step both personally and in my business. If not for my work at Mercy Hospital, I'm not sure I would be a chocolate maker. And if I backed off from some of our initiatives every time things were going well, or poorly, my business wouldn't be where it is today. Keep pressing ahead with your business vocation without expectation of monetary reward or benefit of any kind. That being said, you should create some measures or parameters, including defining "success" of your vocation. You might also, like us, have sustainability parameters for some of your projects. Our school lunch program has a built-in exit plan, so the school will eventually be feeding the students without our help.

Your business vocation is a living organism that is continually open to growth and contraction. Something unexpected is around the next corner. Your vocation of becoming your "authentic self" as a business is never-ending, but the work is your tether that brings you back again and again. This is how you and your business wake up, see more clearly, experience more joy, and day by day uncover your true self. This is why we do what we do. Yes, we want to be financially healthy and this process, paradoxically, makes that possible.

EXERCISES

· ·

How to write your vocation vision of greatness, as adapted from *Zingerman's Guide to Good Leading, Part 3: A Lapsed Anarchist's Approach to Managing Ourselves* (copyright Ari Weinzweig, 2013).

1. Agree on a time frame for your group's vision. For example, are you writing what your vocation will look like in five years? Ten years? You decide how far in the future you want to plan.

2. Find a quiet place where you will be uninterrupted for the next thirty minutes.

3. Review all the material from step 2 above as an accumulation of all the positive possibilities for your company. Alone, grab a pen and paper and take five minutes to write a list of words that first come to mind after you've spent some time reflecting on all of step 2. You can certainly do this in a group if you want to make sure that it happens in the time frame you want, but it's not necessary.

4. Using the "hot pen" technique, write your own draft vocation vision of greatness for twenty minutes without stopping. Write sentences, not outlines and not bullet points. Express your vision in great detail, using all of your senses. Write how you feel about these details. Go for something great. Ari has written extensively on this step and why it's important to dream big and not settle for mediocrity. Once you've completed your draft vision, leave it alone for a couple of days, then revisit it by editing it into a second draft.

5. Assign someone to collect and assimilate the draft visions submitted by your vocation group. This person will prepare a chart with the common themes down the left side and the initials of the vision writers across the top. We also list the themes on the left in order of weight, given the collective drafts from top to bottom. Reviewing each draft, the assimilator will put an X in each box that discusses that theme topic.

6. Make everyone's draft available for reading in a shared folder.

7. The next step is group discussion about the drafts and chart. Although we have not done it this way, Ari suggests that you could give each group member a certain number of votes (using colored dot stickers).

8. Once there is some consensus, you can assign a group member to write the final vocation vision of greatness, which will then be circulated to each member of the group for comment and suggested revision.

9. Depending on your team's level of experience and confidence you might decide to let your trusted advisers read your vision. For example, Askinosie Chocolate had an advisory board for the first five or six years and this would have been something I would have shown them for review and comment.

10. Start living it out! Act on it! Use the document often to guide your actions and bring you closer and closer to the "authentic self" of your business.

CHAPTER 3

....

How Much Is Enough?

The Harmony of Profit and Good Works

The air was thick, but beyond the dirt road that cut through the grounds I noticed the tall grasses swaying. I carefully scooped some rice and the brown, salty beans, called *njano* in Swahili, out of my bowl. I closed my eyes to appreciate the sweetness of the rice. As far as I could see in front of me were children dressed in blue and white, eating the same rice and beans on bright blue plastic plates, and I was reminded of one of my favorite phrases: "It's not about the chocolate, it's about the chocolate." This memory is from several years ago, during an origin trip to Kyela, Tanzania, where we began the second of three sustainable lunch programs in our cocoa partner communities. These are funded by a project we call A Product of Change. I'll come back to this story later.

Throw Out Dualism—It's Time for Unity

In this day and age, most large companies have "corporate social responsibility" (CSR) departments charged with directing philanthropy and other community benefits. This team often operates independently among the typical accounting, marketing, and sales departments. We're accustomed to this organizational compartmentalization because western thought teaches us to keep the parts separate. This dualistic perspective is pervasive in western society: black or white; this or that; and never the two shall meet. CSR departments came to life in the 1960s, mostly staffed by lawyers as risk managers, to anticipate and take action on regulatory and compliance issues before they became a problem. Today, many modern CSR departments act as the "soul" of the company, advancing the mission and engaging in activities that benefit mankind. Criticism of CSR is widespread. There's a business ideology that posits that profit and shareholder value are sacrificed and degraded by CSR activities, while other detractors see CSR as mere window dressing.

We think differently about this kind of compartmentalizing; namely, we disagree with it as it relates to our business. Dualism takes two things and says that they are not related at all; we say they're interdependent. Follow this circle: our chocolate business supports our vocation, and our vocation supports our chocolate business, which supports our vocation. Our aim is to transcend the limiting belief prevalent in traditional business that says "doing good" exists only at the expense of profit. It's not either/or. For us they drive each other and are inseparable. We integrate the notions of our vocation into every department and decision in the company.

What is great chocolate? Is it the chocolate bar itself, or is it something more? We believe great chocolate is the embodiment of a lot of other things. We believe our chocolate is great because of our vocation, which is both our dedication to practicing our craft with excellence and our dedication to serving our team, neighborhood, and origin communities. We want people to buy our chocolate because it tastes good and it tastes good because of our vocation.

Businesses become great or meaningful when they are informed by a vocation that gives their product or service, and their employees, purpose. The vocation is not window dressing for the business. If we pull our "business" apart from our vocation, then it ceases to be great. Great chocolate is a state of character, a way of being, as opposed to a piece of food. If someone mimicked our chocolate bar, with the exact same physical qualities but lacking intention, then I believe it would not be great chocolate.

We are a company resisting the traditional dualistic view that life and business are separate. Instead, they are integrally connected. The quality of our chocolate bar will suffer if we do not recognize this interconnectedness.

We aren't looking to eradicate all imperfection from our product or business, but rather to harmonize the imperfections into our way of being as a company. Also, it's not about striking an exactly equal balance between business and vocation, but about finding harmony in the two concerns, even when they are asymmetrical.

When Did Shopping Become a Way of Life— and a Cure for Our GDP?

Tuesdays with Morrie changed my life. It's the story of a retired professor who is dying of ALS and recounting his life to a former student, now a journalist. At nine years old, Lawren read it aloud to me in the evenings during a time in my life that was challenging, to put it mildly. Let's call it "the beginning of the end of my law career" or "when I finally began grieving my father's death." Anyway, because of this I'm partial to the book and there are several sentiments that to this day strike a chord within me, most of them about death. But there's one chapter in particular where Morrie talks about money.

"We've got a form of brainwashing going on in our country," Morrie sighed. "Do you know how they brainwash people? They repeat something over and over. And that's what we do in this country. Owning things is good. More money is good. More commercialism is good. More is good. More is good. We repeat it—and have it repeated to us—over and over until nobody bothers to think otherwise. . . . You can't substitute material things for love or gentleness or for tenderness or for a sense of comradeship."

Two pages over, Morrie instructs Mitch how to find a meaningful life:

"Devote yourself to loving others, devote yourself to your community around you, and devote yourself to something that gives you purpose and meaning. You notice," he added, grinning, "there's nothing in there about a salary."

Morrie wasn't the first to criticize commercialism and he certainly won't be the last. The brainwashing that Morrie is referring to began after World War II and has been gaining strength since then. We measure a nation's gross domestic product (the sum of all goods and services produced over a period of time) in dollars, then draw conclusions about that nation's general growth, development, and well-being. The health of the American economy, as with much of the globe, is critically dependent on our consumption. Approximately 70 percent of American GDP is consumer spending. This is simply not sustainable.[5]

Many will recall that President Bush encouraged us to shop in the wake of the 9/11 attacks. He was suggesting that we should not let fear

---

5 https://www.stlouisfed.org/publications/regional-economist/january-2012/dont-expect-consumer-spending-to-be-the-engine-of-economic-growth-it-once-was.

keep us from our normal lives. More unfortunate, but understandable, Bush implored Americans to shop as the cloud of the Great Recession was gathering steam in late 2006.[6] So shop we did! To such an extent, in fact, that people died.

In November 2008, Jdimytai Damour was trampled to death at a Walmart on Black Friday. He was trying, along with other employees, to hold back a raucous crowd of shoppers whose sheer force pressing against the glass shattered the doors before the store was set to open at 5:00 a.m.[7] According to a report in the *New York Times*, a witness said, "When they were saying they had to leave, that an employee got killed, people were yelling, 'I've been in line since yesterday morning,'" and she added, "They kept shopping." This incident had a profound impact on me at the time. The stampede was captured on video and is heartbreaking to watch. How could we let this happen? Was it an anomaly or a symbol of a new standard? Unfortunately, this tragedy was not an isolated incident. There is now a website dedicated to tracking deaths and injuries on Black Friday.

American consumer spending as a percentage of GDP is not sustainable for a variety of reasons. Chief among them? Consumption is dependent on debt.[8] Earned income over the last four decades has been stagnant for 90 percent of the lowest wage earners.[9] In the meantime, that income and collateral have secured the increasing debt needed to grow consumer spending. One financial writer argues that paying the

---

6 http://www.nytimes.com/2006/12/20/washington/20text-bush.html: "As we work with Congress in the coming year to chart a new course in Iraq and strengthen our military to meet the challenges of the 21st century, we must also work together to achieve important goals for the American people here at home. This work begins with keeping our economy growing.... And I encourage you all to go shopping more."

7 http://www.nytimes.com/2008/11/29/business/29walmart.html.

8 http://www.oftwominds.com/blogdec13/doomed-consumer12-13.html.

9 Ibid.

growing interest on that debt (which we need to grow the economy) is akin to a snake eating its own tail.[10] Therefore, it's imperative that we find other ways to drive the economy, for the well-being of our families, our employees, and ourselves.

Intentional Consumption

I own a chocolate factory that depends on shoppers who want to *consume* a premium chocolate bar that can cost $10, $15, or more. Who am I to criticize the world's addiction to consumption? Don't I want to sell more chocolate bars? Of course! I want demand for our products! I am, however, advocating for intentional and meaningful consumption. We must become more mindful about the things we purchase or we risk losing sight of what's important until it's beyond our grasp. Do I need it? Why do I want this thing? What is its value? Who made it? Where does it come from? What enjoyment will I derive from it?

What I am not suggesting, though, is an adherence to this ideology that eventually creates the same myopia as thoughtless consumption. The satirical sketch comedy show *Portlandia* does a great job of exposing the dangers (and annoyances) of this misguided approach. There's one episode in particular at the (now closed) Gilt Club restaurant. The waitress, cross-examined about the chicken by Fred and Carrie, reports that "Colin" was in fact a Heritage breed, fed a diet of sheep's milk, soy, and hazelnuts. Fred and Carrie decide to leave the restaurant in midorder, after examining his "papers," and visit the "local" chicken farm to personally verify the waitress's claims. It was hilarious and a great reminder of the balance required in our decision-making process. There's consumption for consumption's sake, and then there's consumption that's *so* thoughtful it consumes the consumer. As entrepreneurs we have a duty to find a way to encourage mindful consumption of our products.

10 Ibid.

Greatness and Goodness—Embrace the Harmony

All business vocations should strive for greatness (excellence—quality) and goodness (heart). All business vocations should have a harmony between profit and the desire to do good work for the world.

How do you achieve this? By pursuing both priorities all the time. In practice, this means that one priority may "win out" over another depending on the situation. And therein lies a natural tension. A good tension. It will exist at every level of the organization and your job is to embrace it, while also managing employees or colleagues on both ends of the spectrum. These seemingly opposing camps contribute to an important asymmetry in your organization, which you need. Why, you might ask, do you need asymmetry? To me, it's kind of like wabi-sabi, the Japanese design aesthetic based on the beauty of imperfection. Instead of being distracted by a quest for ever-elusive balance, and therefore shutting off other possibilities, we seek out the imperfect, jagged edges of business life, and find greater creativity in asymmetry. The harmony between profit and service to the community should be pursued wholeheartedly, in spite of its challenges. With some practice, you'll learn to embrace those challenges as opportunities for growth. Ultimately each situation is analyzed as a "business decision," meaning that if we're not operating from excellence first, then we won't have a business through which to do good works. Later in this chapter, I'll give an example of what it looks like when one priority wins over another.

If your company wants to serve the community and you want the best product possible, then feel free to steal our mantra, "It's not about the chocolate, it's about the chocolate." This confounding statement is at the center of who we are as a company. Seeking a transformed heart, working with students in our neighborhood, finding kinship—these things are not about the chocolate. They are about living a meaningful life. On the other hand, they are totally about the chocolate. We must make the best chocolate we can possibly make by laser-focusing on taste, quality, flavor, texture, and the overall experience. We fiercely compete year after year to win awards for the quality of our chocolate. Do you think people would buy our chocolate more than once if it tasted like sawdust? No way! And we wouldn't want them to! We don't want people buying our chocolate because they feel sorry for our farmers or want to support our projects with a chocolate purchase, regardless of its quality. We hope people purchase our chocolate primarily because they think it's a great product; then we hope the more folks learn about what we do, the better they feel about their purchase. We tell our story so you can hear it and be inspired to care about something, anything, in your own life or business. We want our story to prompt the thought: *Where's my kinship? If they can do it, I can, too!* That's our goal.

What's Your Growth Strategy?

"Grow or die," say the business school professors and consultants. Typically, that means grow sales, net operating income, market share, and on and on. This is a seductive premise and a fundamental mistake at the core of most organizations. Often accelerated by the desire for more, more, more, this canon of "successful" business is potentially harmful. The harm is that *more* can come with a sacrifice; growth but at what cost? So then how does Askinosie Chocolate grow? We constantly ask, Is this enough? We define growth more broadly than the traditional business world. A changed heart, interior peace, higher-quality products, reduced debt, more efficient work flow, higher pay for staff, and the like will transform us little by little and that's the kind of growth we hope never ceases.

Speaking of interior peace, I was inspired to ponder this question of "What is enough?" from my relationship with Assumption Abbey monastery (yes, the one I mentioned at the beginning of this book). Maximizing sales growth is not something you typically hear in a monastery and it's all because of the Rule of Benedict. The Rule of Benedict is the oldest organizational management document in history. Broken into numbered sections, it has governed the day-to-day operations of monasteries and convents since the sixth century. While it's true that the monks live in community, do not own property, and live a vow of poverty, they are also economically self-sufficient. They do not rely on charity to survive; they don't even accept "charity"—it's contrary to the Rule, which governs their life in community and individually. They want to be self-sufficient. Many people aren't aware of this. They balance life with daily work, prayer, and biblical reading: *ora, labora et lectio.* Every monastery has an income-producing activity—anything from farming to cheese making, baking, or art—but importantly they follow Rule of Benedict 57, which states:

> 1 If there are artisans in the monastery, they are to practice their craft with all humility, but only with the abbot's permission. 2 If one of them becomes puffed up by his skillfulness in his craft, and feels that he is conferring something on the monastery, 3 he is to be removed from practicing his craft and not allowed to resume it unless, after manifesting his humility, he is so ordered by the abbot. 4 Whenever products of these artisans are sold, those responsible for the sale must not dare to practice any fraud. 5 Let them always remember Ananias and Sapphira, who incurred bodily death (Acts 5:1–11), 6 lest they and all who perpetrate fraud in monastery affairs suffer spiritual death. 7 The evil of avarice must have no part in establishing prices, 8 which should, therefore, always be a little lower than people outside the monastery are able to set, 9 so that in all things God may be glorified (1 Pet 4:11).

This Rule is dense, but there are some key concepts for the success of 1,500 years of monastic life and business. Monasteries are particularly mindful of pricing to avoid over- or underpricing. They don't want to hurt their neighbors who might be selling a similar product.

I have personally experienced this Rule at Assumption Abbey, where I am a family brother. Recently, the abbey monks sewed some small cloth bags for us to use as packaging for a chocolate project. Determining the price per unit that they would charge us was not an easy task. They went to great lengths so as not to overcharge us, even though it was a relatively small amount of money. Last Christmas, we decided to sell the abbey's fruitcakes in our factory storefront. I told my spiritual director last year that the abbey should raise the price, that people would pay more, that they were worth more, and he politely restated the Rule explaining that would not be possible. Oh, yeah. Oops. He told me what I already know: that the abbey only needs to make "enough" income. In fact, it's more basic than that. Do you know how many fruitcakes the abbey makes per year? Enough. Enough for the abbey to survive. This is true for Benedictine Rule monasteries and convents around the world. This notion is best explained by the abbot of the Saint Sixtus Abbey of Westvleteren in Belgium, famous for its Trappist beer: "We are not brewers. We are monks. We brew beer to be able to afford being monks."[11] Demand far outpaces production, but they only make enough. They possess a keen sense of what enough means.

We're not monks, but this encapsulates the Askinosie Chocolate philosophy, too. However, ours is circular. Our vocation supports the business and the business supports our vocation, in harmony. They support and depend on each other. We're in constant pursuit of both profitability (business) and kinship (vocation) and they both make our chocolate better. We can afford the community engagement work we do because—and only because—we firstly make great chocolate that people want to buy and enjoy.

---

11 http://query.nytimes.com/gst/fullpage.html?res=9403E1DE153EF931A2575BC0A9639C8B63.

What is enough for you? Enough of what? This is a moving target with dynamic answers. Keep asking this question with discipline and adherence to your vision and vocation and you will experience joy tempered with a tinge of stress with the answer: "Yes, this is enough!" The root of this question is also the central theme of the Rule of Benedict: humility.

The best example of the "enough" analysis is revenue and net operating income. Do we have enough of both? Enough for what? At our company we have financial goals that include higher wages and salaries for our workers, reduced debt, and some cushion for equipment maintenance and replacement. The answer is that we do not yet have enough revenue and net operating income in order to achieve all of those goals. We know where we need to be and how to get there. I don't have any partners, venture capital, or investors and while it would be easy to raise funds that way, it's not necessary to accomplish our goals. We are intentionally small and operate from cash flow. So we grow in order to have enough for our vision of the company. While slowly increasing revenue and net income, we remain focused on other aspects of growth.

It's not our goal to be the biggest chocolate company in the world. We'll leave that to others. It will be enough for us that we're known as the best-tasting direct trade chocolate available.

ASKINOSIE CHOCOLATE TOUCHSTONE: HOW WE DEFINE "ENOUGH"

The answer to the question "What is enough?" will be different for every company. Ours is dependent on several factors, most of which is outlined in our vision, such as our growth strategy, my personal financial wants and needs, and the wants and needs of our employees. "Enough" can also be a moving target. We have several "enoughs" involving our staff, our product, and our brand. When you arrive at enough, it's not as though you cease your efforts; you continue striving for excellence and may choose to set the bar elsewhere. Our first "enough" goal was to pay all our employees a living wage. Once we achieved that, we didn't stop giving raises or bonuses. Our overall "enough" is to be widely known as the best-tasting direct trade chocolate in the world. We're still working on that one.

Defining and Measuring "Enough"

As a leader of a small company my main goal is both human and financial. I want financial health as I've defined it above, *and* I want to change my heart. I want a business that is an ecosystem in which hearts can change. We strive for a workplace where the pursuit of interior peace is possible. For example, we intentionally have very few people who work over forty hours per week. We have some overtime, but it's limited. It's not that we don't want to pay it, but that we want people to rest and have time with family. We do everything we can to have an orderly workflow without big swings of hurry-up-and-wait. It's something that we talk about every week.

While we have yet to use a survey, it would be feasible and useful. You could survey before implementing your business vocation to obtain a baseline response. With a few simple questions you could follow the transformation of hearts over time. You could also assess the rate of adoption, i.e., participation in vocational projects over time, and gauge satisfaction (as long as managers do not force or expect participation). The temptation will be to look at short-term productivity or profitability as a benchmark. While there's nothing wrong with analysis of correlations, it would be important to look at the long view before making conclusions about causation.

What if your workplace is simply too large for you to discern your employees' emotional lives? I would break it down into manageable parts. What is happening at the work group or team level? This is not a lean manufacturing issue that can be addressed on a gemba walk around the factory floor, along the hospital hallways, or among the rows of cubicles to observe people at work. Team leaders need to be able to feel the successes, and struggles, of the active business vocation, just like I do leading our factory of sixteen people. Most teams and work groups are this size. It's no surprise that small military units have been formally organized and used since Napoleon. A squad leader, for example, will always know what is happening among the small group he or she is leading. That leader will report up the chain of command. This is simple stuff. You, as the leader, want to know when your employees' kids are sick, what challenges they may be facing, what ideas they have for improvement, where they would like to contribute to the vocation and vision of the business. This is basic human engagement and relationship building. And it pays dividends toward the business vocation and the bottom line.

The gemba walk takes on added meaning for me. It's more like a crawl because observing the "real place" takes time, compassion, and mutuality. I am in the factory, all corners of it, almost every day. I have a pattern: first, to the packaging room to talk to Flora and her team; then to Russell at the butter press; then to Kevin in the roasting room; then to the molding room to see Brad; then to storefront retail; and finally, shipping. My cubicle is down the street, where our office is located. We have open offices, so I'm among our other departments (sales and marketing) all day long. I talk with our chief kinship officer regularly about our integrated kinship needs, Chocolate University, and concerns and possible action steps. One of my intentions with my version of the gemba walk is to look for outliers. Who is opting out of team lunches? Who is not participating or interacting? Who is speaking up in the huddle? I am noticing the spirit and energy people bring to our environment. If you're an openhearted leader, then you'll know how people are interacting at work. You'll know which workers are sharing, collaborating, and displaying empathy, humility, and interdependence. You'll watch out for, encourage, and protect employees' awareness of their place in the whole, and whether they view the work as bigger than themselves. Lawren works remotely, but she has her own version of a gemba walk. She picks up the phone and talks to each person on her small sales and marketing team almost every day.

Staying closely connected with our colleagues and employees helps us to measure what "enough" means for much of our work. For example, we measure debt reduction. We measure quality by carefully taste-testing our products each week. We discuss peaceful workflow with Brad, our production manager, each week in production meetings. Higher pay for staff is an agenda item at nearly all finance meetings and we monitor our progress over time. We're tempted by the lure of additional equipment with higher capacities, allowing us to make significantly more chocolate. If we invest X amount of capital then it will give us Y capacity increase, but in order to invest we need to borrow. Here lies the deceivingly shiny lure, but we know it hides a hook that can cause pain for us if we don't carefully analyze how the decision fits with our vision and vocation for our company. All decisions, big and small, should be filtered through those ideals by asking, "Will this help us reach our goals, according to our vision and vocation?"

Four Concrete Methods to Measure "Enough" in Any Business

1. **Based on impact:** This method measures the number of people or groups of people affected by the work. For example, we can measure impact by households supported: farmers (1 household), full-time employees (1 household), students at A Product of Change schools (0.2 or 0.3 households). We then

measure these numbers over time. "Enough" could be the maintenance or growth of these numbers over time or the mix of the numbers organized in a desired way. For example, if my company grows, then I would want to measure the ratio of company employees to households affected. This kind of measurement is key in larger companies or high-growth businesses because it's easy to lose track of impact over time.

2. **Based on objective:** Measure advancement toward an objective over time. For example, suppose our objective is to eradicate malnutrition in the schools, with the nutrition programs we have founded. We can measure the percentage of malnourished students (as defined by the World Health Organization) along with test scores and attendance. "Enough" is when the objective is met. Our progress for Enlightened Boys and Empowered Girls may be measured by total boys and girls going on to university.

3. **Based on project sustainability:** Here I am going to borrow from Christian tradition to discuss the allocation of time, talent, and treasure. Consideration of these three T words is important to us as we plan a new project: We estimate the hours in a week or month it will take to execute the project. We assess the skill set or talent required to manage it. Finally, we look at the "treasure," or the funding over the life of the project. Over time the balance of time, talent, and treasure of social projects should shift to favor the recipient organization. None of these measures should begin as a single source, meaning they should not all originate from just one of the parties, but from both. One group should not contribute all of the time, talent, or money to make the project work. In order to establish a sustainable focused partnership, both parties should be on board for all of those measures. "Enough" is the delicate balance of time, talent, and treasure to

create a sustainable model. Additionally, we want to see impact without undue burden on either organization. For example, we want to start an Empowered Girls project where the students make soap—they want to create a model for life skills development and profit. The girls make soap with their time and talent; we provide start-up supplies and equipment; then, through their sales, they are able to fund the supplies themselves. The same is true for A Product of Change models we've started for school lunches in Tanzania and the Philippines; the parent-teacher association of each school invests time and talent and some treasure (product) and we provide time and talent. Gradually we shift the amounts to favor the PTA.

4. **Based on vision of change:** This idea of measure is a composite that builds a total picture of change. Using the vision established for an organization or project, we can assign measures of success then track along the way to meet vision. For the Mababu, Tanzania, farmers' vision, this might include the percentage of families who send their children to school, the percentage of households with year-round food security or electricity, and/or the percentage of co-op farmer members with computer training.

HOW DEFINING "ENOUGH" INFLUENCES YOUR GROWTH STRATEGY

Let's use the example of a bread delivery truck. If I buy a delivery van for $15,000 to start my business and at the end of the year I have $10,000 of net income, then I have a 66 percent return on asset ($10,000 divided by $15,000). I decide that I don't have enough [fill in the blank] so I buy another delivery van for my bread business for $15,000. At the end of the year I have $18,000 in net income and so I have a 60 percent return on asset ($18,000 divided by $30,000); 6 percent less than when I only had one van. This can get very complicated in a hurry, but you get the point. Perhaps I am willing to invest in the added delivery van because I need it to have more capacity for enough sales to achieve X, or I believe that the value of my company is not enough and more sales will improve it. The list of reasons is long. However, it might also be a mistake because we have not defined what "enough" means to our business. "Grow or die" is a siren song for most of us and if you're not careful then get ready for the possible pain of cash flow shortages when it's time to make the payments required for the new delivery truck. It's called undercapitalization.

Not All Employees Think Like All Other Employees: The Beauty of Vocation Tension

"How do you deal with employees and colleagues who don't connect with the social justice aspect of the business?" This is a question I hear frequently. I've got good news and bad news. The good news? You don't just "deal with" those colleagues. The bad news (or the difficult news, really)? You need to embrace, appreciate, and learn from the dialogue. This can be uncomfortable because vocations are personal, but this is very important.

On one end of the spectrum we have people in our company who come to work excited to do their job because they are supporting smallholder cocoa farmers across the globe or helping feed malnourished children. They care deeply about that and they feel it imbues their job with more meaning. On the other end of the spectrum, we have employees who don't care as much about the fact that we engage with neighborhood students in our Chocolate University program, or at least they aren't as motivated by it. They want to practice their craft. The important point is: both types of employees contribute to the spectrum and tension, which we need. Those people on the far ends, pulling for their side, are advocating for important things and we must listen to them. They both care deeply about the company.

It's possible that we have had employees over the years who do not care deeply about anything but a paycheck. These people eventually weed themselves out of the company. We're not offering a one-size-fits-all model. In some cases, the tension has even been between me and my wife, whose judgment I trust. For example, in the very early years she asked: "Why are we sharing profits with farmers when it does not seem to make any difference to them or in the quality of cocoa beans we are receiving?" She was right that it wasn't initially clear if the farmers cared about the profit-sharing model. At first, that question upset me; it felt like a criticism of direct trade and, in a way, of my vision for the company. I was defensive, lashing out with retorts like, "Because I told them we would. Is that good enough for you?" Over time, as I gained confidence and knowledge, I wasn't defensive anymore, and I saw how that and other questions helped me clarify and improve my thinking and my business practices.

"It's not about the chocolate, it's about the chocolate" is very real. It's not about the chocolate, it's about our relationship with farmers, it's about sharing. At the same time, it *is* about the chocolate, the quality of the beans, and the attention to every single detail that makes it one of the best bars in the world. This is why the tension not only works but is a key ingredient in our success. The differing opinions of our leadership team are grounding in an organization where grounding is crucial to success. Sometimes Lawren and I strongly disagree about sales and marketing issues, and it's neither subtle nor quiet. This is probably common in family businesses. I've come to heavily rely on her instinct (and her dissent) in every aspect of the business. The struggle to balance the priorities of profit and good works is a worthy pursuit, because it's in that process that great decisions are made for the future of our company. When you're trying to achieve harmony, though, there will be tension. And that's okay. It's a daily process; there are daily choices to make. But with your business vocation in mind, your vision of greatness, and even your measurements of "enough," the choice won't be as difficult as you may think. Our vocation is visualized as a circle (our chocolate business supports our vocation, and our vocation supports our chocolate business, which supports our vocation), but there is still a spectrum upon which the preferences of those in your organization fall. On one end of the spectrum is dedication to good works and on the other end is dedication to craft, excellence, and profitability.

Balancing the Spectrum: Where Great Decisions Are Made

My business, like most, is not a democracy, but I need to support civil disagreement among team members. If I don't encourage dissent in my day-to-day vocational life of business activities then there will come a day when none of my employees say what they really think. If that happens, then we need to prepare for eventual failure because it's not possible to be right all of the time.

The Rule of Benedict 3 specifically addresses the importance of hearing all voices in the monastery when decisions must be made:

Whenever any important business has to be done in the monastery, let the abbot call together the whole community and state the matter to be acted upon. Then, having heard the brethren's advice, let him turn the matter over in his own mind and do what he shall judge to be most expedient. The reason we have said that all should be called for counsel is that the Lord often reveals to the younger what is best.

It's fascinating that 1,500 years ago the management document of the monastic institutions that would one day usher in advancements in agriculture, art, and industry accounted for young monks' counsel on important matters. At the factory we are guided by this Rule and we seek the wisdom of the entire group of employees on important matters, especially big purchases. It's natural for us since we practice open-book management and share finances weekly with everyone in our company. Further, because we teach what the numbers mean we can get great input from the group. Like the monasteries, I seek input from everyone, listen, then make the best decision for the good of the company. Under the Rule, the abbot is obliged to manage the abbey in such a way that young monks can speak their mind without intimidation. This cannot be accomplished if dissent is discouraged into silence. So embrace the tension, encourage employees on both ends of the spectrum to speak their minds, and be willing to approach it all with humility.

The fundamental point is that the resulting decisions, born of tension and dissent, are what propels our company into sustainability, and that, moreover, this is the place where creativity reigns. It is within this transcendence of "either/or" dualism that greatness and even transformation can at times occur.

A Product of Change:
Vocation Tension in Real Life

Here is what harmonizing profit and good works looks like in practice. What follows is an example of when I was faced with the difficult business decisions we entrepreneurs are faced with all the time. Do you remember my story at the beginning of this chapter? Well, let me explain about that meal, that school, and why I was there.

A couple of years ago we ordered fifteen metric tons of cocoa beans from our Tanzanian farmer group. We also ordered one thousand bags (one metric ton) of rice from the PTA at Mwaya Secondary School, one of the poorest-performing schools in Tanzania, located in the area where we purchase beans. Both the beans and the rice were supposed to be loaded on our container leaving Dar es Salaam, Tanzania, bound for our factory in Springfield, Missouri. We use the cocoa beans to . . . ding, ding, ding—make chocolate! As for the rice? We sell it in our store and online and all of the proceeds fund lunch for about one thousand Mwaya students, every school day, for a year. The rice is a naturally sweet, medium-grain rice and is the best rice I've ever tasted (and man, I've had a lot of rice). It's so good, in fact, that *Bon Appétit* has called it a "pantry staple."

We have three of these sustainable lunch programs at present: one at Mwaya Secondary in Kyela, Tanzania; one at Malagos Elementary in Davao, Philippines; and a new one at Baguio Central Elementary also in Davao. The idea for the programs originated on one of my trips to Davao in 2011. While visiting our cocoa farmer partners, I stopped by Malagos Elementary School because I was interested in partnering with a local school. Originally we had some educational initiatives (like bringing Internet and laptops to the school, through the work of one of our local Chocolate University schools in Springfield), but when the principal told me she had many malnourished students I knew we needed to do more. Together we decided to address the nutritional needs of the students. The result is what we call "A Product of Change." The school PTA (yes, there are PTAs in the jungle and the parent participation is higher than at most schools I know of in the United States) produces Tableya, a traditional Filipino hot cocoa drink made from disks of ground cocoa beans. This Tableya makes a hot, frothy, deeply chocolaty drink that is both delicious and full of antioxidants. The PTA packages it and puts it on our container of cocoa beans bound for our factory. We sell the Tableya for $10 and that $10 will provide 150 meals for the students. It's important to note that in each of these programs lunch is provided for *all* the students, not just those who are wasted or severely wasted.

Since June 2011 we've sent sales proceeds to the school monthly and they source local food, which is prepared by PTA volunteers every day. In every case, we are simply providing the schools access to market. Before each program begins, and throughout the duration of the year, we monitor the height and weight of all students so we can measure the success of the program. We also monitor attendance, grades, and test scores, all of which we're proud to report have been positively affected by the school lunches. As of 2016, the rate of malnutrition at Malagos Elementary in the Philippines dropped to zero (measured by wasting, per UN standards).

Sustainability Means Planning an Exit Strategy

We recently challenged Malagos to locate another nearby school in need and coach that school in the implementation of a similar program. At that point, the program at Malagos had been going on for five years and the teachers and parents at Malagos were experts. They formed a committee, developed a how-to manual, and met with counterparts at the nearby Baguio Central School.[12] After several months of work and before we kicked off the program at Baguio, I met with teachers and administrators of the school. It was amazing to see how organized, active, and passionate the parents and teachers were. This is not always the case. They followed our guidelines on how to make the Tableya to

---

12 Malagos drafted a workbook detailing the steps necessary to implement A Product of Change lunch program. Specifically, the school has established an organizational structure of both parent and teacher committees, which are integral to the success of the lunch program, addressing financial management, reporting, food buying, and data collection on student nutrition (measured by wasting rates). Drawing from this module and from its experience managing this program in the Philippines and Tanzania, we assisted in the formulation of a budget for daily lunches, monitoring monthly expenses to ensure available funding, promote cooperation between parents and teachers celebrating successes, regularly communicate with a school liaison, and provide structure controls to prevent corruption and theft. We will also monitor school reports of attendance and test score results.

meet our specifications, to ensure we have a high-quality product to sell. The plan is—and has always been—that we will withdraw from Malagos at the end of five years and remain in partnership with them on other programs, but not school lunch because the participants can stand on their own and provide for the kids without us. Because we've been creating a demand for their product, and they've been learning along the way, Malagos is more than prepared to take this program entirely into its own hands.

This is what true sustainability looks like. It's my belief that the school will keep feeding the children and my hope that the PTA and students will not remember me or my company ten years from now; at least, not for having anything to do with their school lunch program. This is important because it's our partners who are the solution, not Askinosie Chocolate. Of course our relationship with the PTA, teachers, and students is paramount, as we see ourselves in kinship with them. To that end, we will not put our desire for friendship in front of our intention to be part of the solution. In other words, we would not be very good friends if we encouraged our partners to depend on us for funding in perpetuity. Building this empowerment is more arduous than supplying an infinite checkbook but so much more rewarding—and productive. Finally, sustainability relates to our organizational humility. On one hand, it feels good to know that someone depends on us. On the other hand, a community partner's long-term dependence on us can be unhealthy. Of course there are exceptions to this notion, but we are not indispensable and should not act as if we are.

Mwaya, the school in Tanzania, has about one thousand students as well, but the malnourishment was even more pronounced there. Every student was eating only one meal per day. Like in the Davao program, we had an existing relationship with this school and as we deepened our relationship, we became more aware of the malnutrition and its tragic effects. Girls were selling themselves for food, getting pregnant, and being forced out of school. Some girls faced unsafe and illegal abortions.

I mentioned earlier this was one of the poorest-performing schools in Tanzania. Well, it was actually at the very bottom of the list. It was the number one worst-performing school in the country. We knew malnutrition contributed to this greatly, so we partnered with the PTA of this school. It's important, again, to recognize the commitment of the parents, many of whom travel to meetings at the school by bicycle from a great distance on what you and I would definitely not call a road. I once called a PTA meeting at a school near our factory in Springfield (where malnourishment is also a tragic issue, yet people are less willing or able to see it) to discuss a possible nutrition program for their kids.... Five people showed up.

In our sustainable lunch program at Mwaya, we buy this amazingly delicious rice, packaged in kilo bags, one thousand bags at a time. They load them on our cocoa bean container and we sell them for $16.50 each—that money provides 210 meals. As in Davao, we monitor height, weight, school performance, etc. We're getting close to our handoff of this lunch program as well. And again, as in Davao, the school is ready. They're prepared. We're happy to report that only a few students of the seven hundred are below the normal health line and school attendance has risen from 55 percent in 2012 to 85 percent in 2017.[13]

That Time I Left a Metric Ton of Cocoa Beans Behind to Make Room for Rice

Now, back to my story of balancing the tension of profit and good works and the time when profit gave way. The Tanzania farmers trucked the fifteen metric tons of cocoa beans we had ordered on a twenty-two-hour journey to the port of Dar es Salaam and delivered it to the exporter's warehouse for packing on the shipping container. They also

---

13 Convoy of Hope 2016 Mwaya Impact Report, Daudi Msseemmaa, Africa/Asia field director.

packed up the metric ton of rice. Did I mention that I had paid for the beans? The problem was that they could not fit all of the bags of beans *and* all of the rice onto the twenty-foot container. Despite multiple assurances to the contrary, it was not all going to fit.

One choice would have been to leave the rice behind and offer it to the students for food to eat at school. That was not really a choice. The reason? The leverage of the American marketplace. If we left the rice behind for meals, then the school would have roughly 35,000 meals of just rice. If we bring that same rice to America, sell it as we do, and return the money to the school, then we fund about 210,000 meals with that same metric ton of rice. The success of this program is about leverage.

I needed the cocoa beans to make chocolate to sell because, well, that is how we survive as a company. I had to make a quick decision about what to do. Securing a forty-foot container was out of the question due to the high cost. I had to have the rice because we'd promised the school that we would sell the rice and fund the school lunch program with the proceeds. Air freight was out of the question and my options were narrowing fast. I consulted our leadership team. We e-mailed, researched, racked our brains, and, in the end, decided to leave the near metric ton of cocoa beans behind to make room for the rice. I tried for months to sell the cocoa beans, but when that didn't work we simply gave them back to the farmers. We had already paid for the beans, but this way they could sell them again to someone else in the village. It was a gift of goodwill. They were very appreciative, but felt bad for our predicament. Was this an easy choice? Yes and no. Of course we wanted to do everything we could to try to fit the beans on the container. But once it was clear that we couldn't keep both, everyone, including me, knew that we would leave the beans behind. We'd made a commitment and we intended to keep it. It was the right thing to do. Practically speaking, it built trust and goodwill. By keeping our promises, the community felt more incentivized to keep theirs to us: supply us with excellent cocoa beans. There was mutuality. In the end, it was the right choice and everyone in our factory felt good about it.

The principles of healthy finance and doing good works are so entangled they are not easy to untie and it's probably better that way. They're intertwined organically and authentically. It's not as if we had a philanthropy or "outreach" department we needed to check with to see what they would think about us leaving the rice behind in Dar es Salaam. The thread of making great chocolate and not losing money was and is wrapped around the thread of doing the right thing and honoring promises. We could have made a lot of money on that one metric ton of cocoa beans by turning it into chocolate. Instead, we chose to make room for the one metric ton of rice and sustainably fund about 210,000 lunches at the school—that's about one thousand students (the student population fluctuates) eating lunch every school day. Faced with this classic Kobayashi Maru scenario (for the uninitiated: this term comes from *Star Trek*, and means a no-win situation that tests one's character) we decided that profit would give way to a promise. When your business lives its vocation, then this choice is inescapable.

Third Time's a Charm and So Is Making Payroll

All vocations should have a tension between greatness (excellence—quality) and goodness (heart). It's truly a poetic sentiment that in reality sometimes affects net operating cash flow. We spend real money, not just time, on community development, farmer profit sharing, Chocolate University, and many other projects that are inextricably bound to our vocation of making great chocolate. If we count the hours we spend on these projects—and we don't—then the dollar expense would be much greater. As I look back over ten years of living the day-to-day of this vocation, the work has never prevented us from making payroll. Skeptics would argue that we could have done other things with the money or time, that the opportunity cost has been significant. But we don't see it that way, because we believe all of this makes our chocolate better.

It's worth noting that it's not always Candyland around here. Sometimes we argue; sometimes we take on opportunities that, despite our best efforts, fail. And even though there's growth, it doesn't mean we have fewer worries. When revenue increases it doesn't necessarily mean that things are easier. The Notorious B.I.G. was right when he said, "Mo money, mo problems." It's sometimes—heck, it's often—messy, complicated, and stressful, otherwise known by entrepreneurs as "challenging opportunities." This exercise in vocational business life is not about achieving the perfect balance between profitability and good works, it's about both at the same time. It's about embracing the tension that occurs when you're in pursuit of harmony. That's what we mean when we say, "It's not about the chocolate, it's about the chocolate."

If I asked my friend Ari Weinzweig, "How much is enough?" he would have an answer. But I don't have to ask him because I know what he'd say: First, look at our ten-year vision of greatness, the details of what our company will be like in ten years. Second, here is where our vision says we hope to be financially. We can tie the financial numbers directly to the vision. Our vision story itself is all about what is "enough" and that keeps us on course as opposed to the seduction of more, more, more.

This practice of enough greatness and goodness rests on what St. Augustine called "disordered loves." I heard *New York Times* columnist David Brooks talk about this on a podcast and it resonated with me deeply:

And so I go to Augustine's concept of "disordered loves," which is, we all love a lot of things, and we all know some loves are higher than others. Our love of truth should be higher than our love of money, but because of some screw-up in our nature, we get our loves out of order all the time. So if a friend blabs to you a secret and you tell it at a dinner party, you're putting your love of popularity above your love of friendship, and that's a sin.[14]

My prayer is that we "order our loves" daily at Askinosie Chocolate in a way that honors our vocation. It helps if we've defined it, talked about it, agreed upon it, and celebrated it when we get it right. When I can order my loves in a way that aligns with my life and vocation, I can begin to consider what is enough. This path is not possible without humility. Arrogance will be the ultimate undoing of my venture. Arrogance blinds me from seeing what enough looks like, and believe me, I am blind plenty of days. I will highlight in chapter 5 how to seek out those days of ordered loves, find them, and hold them as best you can as a treasure. A treasure that is perhaps the ultimate "enough."

I love reading anything by visionary Seth Godin. I read one blog every day without fail: his. He inimitably tackles the issue of "enough" by concluding that we are confused. He posits that watching people at work would lead us to think that we never have enough likes, market share, etc. Yet when we watch people at rest we never seem to have "enough things to entertain us," frequently only "shallow friendships, conspicuous displays of success." Then he holds the mirror up for me to see myself: "Lots of us walk around thinking we do have enough education, exposure to difficult topics, situations where we need to change our mind, silence, deep relationships based on trust and commitment. I'm wondering what happens if we flip them?"[15] This chapter is about mitigating our confusion about having enough of the things that matter most.

Below are some exercises that will help you identify "enough" within your organization. All of this should be considered within the

---

14 http://www.onbeing.org/program/david-brooks-and-ej-dionne-sinfulness-hopefulness-and-the-possibility-of-politics/transcript.

15 http://sethgodin.typepad.com/seths_blog/2016/11/the-confusion-about-enough.html.

framework of the business vocation and vision you've created. Whether considering opportunities, assessing challenges, or adjusting "enough" expectations, the business vocation and ultimately the vision should be the touchstone to which you always return. Ask yourself: does this work toward achieving the plans laid out in my vision and does it support the vocation of the company?

EXERCISES

1. Would your company benefit strategically by taking measures to mitigate the effects of the consumption economy? What could you do to encourage intentional consumption?

2. Alone, or in discussion with your leadership team, describe an example of a product or service you offer that is at the pinnacle of greatness. Then describe a counterforce that causes tension, pulling you or the company toward a good thing or project that you're working on. In other words, do you have a cocoa-beans-versus-rice story of your own? How did you resolve the apparent conflict? Can you imagine other stories like this in the life of your business?

3. How would you measure your vocational projects? Would you use the method that's based on impact, objective, project sustainability, or vision of change (or all four) to determine what is "enough"?

4. Can you tie financial goals to your "enough" threshold? In other words, if you reach a financial goal of X, then where would you use that money in order to say "that's enough"? Let's

say you have a target of 10 percent operating cash flow margin. Once you hit that goal, what are the plans for the money?

5. On the flip side, do you have other concepts of "enough" that aren't financial? I mentioned that we strive for emotional or spiritual fulfillment in various ways at our factory. What other values do you want to encourage in your organization, that can be measured? Identifying these values will also help you answer questions 3 and 4 above.

6. Think of an example where you've not only listened to dissenting views in your company but actually encouraged dissent. How did you handle it? Ask other members of your leadership team how you respond to views that are contrary to yours. Do you tend to be defensive? Are you open and encouraging? Do you have a venue for opposing views?

7. Look at your business vocation—where is your company succeeding in living out "enough" as it relates to a tenet of your vocation? How can you make this even more successful in the future? And remember, that doesn't (probably) mean bigger, faster, more.

8. Do you regularly take gemba walks? If not, take one now. Make it your own. How will you observe the changed hearts in your company?

9. Are there examples of "disordered loves" in your company? Go back to your business vocation—what are your priorities? What steps does leadership need to take to reorder them? And how will you exemplify this and then implement it top down within your company?

....

CHAPTER 4

Essentials to Success

Direct Trade and Open-Book Management

When we began purchasing cocoa from the Mababu farmer group in Tanzania, most of them had never tasted chocolate. It's sad, but true. They were harvesting a commodity, until we came along. Seven years later, they're cocoa bean experts. Although their Trinitario beans were good from the beginning, since our relationship began we've worked together on organic practices, proper pruning, intercropping, and post-harvest and fermentation techniques—all of which contribute to an outstanding cocoa bean and a stellar chocolate bar. We perform cut tests and test moisture content. We prioritize education and cocoa bean collaboration to the extent that, while I'm at origin, I'll roast beans over a fire for us to taste-test together. Our farmer partners are true artisans and true partners in direct trade with us. They want to give us better cocoa because they know that we will come back again, that we pay a high price for quality, that we profit share, and that we care about them. A couple of years ago we won a silver medal at the

International Chocolate Awards for our 72 percent Mababu, Tanzania, Dark Chocolate Bar. We had a beach party with our farmers to celebrate this distinction and presented them with a plaque to commemorate the honor. The news was a surprise to the group and they celebrated with clapping, cheering, and yelling. After a few moments the noise died down; I will never forget when the chairwoman, Mamma Mpoki, stood up with a twinkle in her eye and asked me, "What do we need to do to win gold?"

A Better Way

We've all been conditioned—corporations and consumers alike—to pay very little for things we want without a second thought about why or how they're so cheap. If we want things, we need to pay adequately for them. And if we want nice things, well, then we should pay more. The American craft chocolate bar at $10 is a great value and no, you're not being fooled by companies charging that—or more—for it. You are, however, being fooled by companies charging $1 for a chocolate bar. Global context is imperative. Everything has a price. Direct trade and open-book management help us understand the good, the bad, and the ugly of that fact and provide a better way of doing things.

The story above is, simply put, why we practice direct trade. The experience was one of the great "aha" moments of my career and is not entirely dissimilar to when a jury came back with "not guilty." But this was different. It was the result of an intentional and careful collaboration. And although we have yet to win gold, you can bet we're working on it, together.

This story is a result of direct trade, but it's also a by-product of open-book management, of which I've been a devotee for more than twenty years. I began sharing and teaching the numbers when I had my law practice; so there was no question that it would be an integral part of the new chocolate business. Jack Stack, the founding father of open-book management, believes that if employees share in the profits and the outcome of a company's success, they will feel greater ownership in the process leading up to the end result—in our case, a bar of chocolate. For employees to be invested and interested means a better experience for them and better chocolate for us all to enjoy.

The practice of open-book management contains three core concepts:

1. Know and teach the rules. This can be any set of critical numbers that are important to the business. This could be very basic, like sales by month. It could be more complicated, like net operating income. Teaching what these numbers mean and what influences them is key.

2. Follow the action and keep score. This means reporting the numbers at regular meetings. For us, this occurs every Tuesday in a huddle with all employees present (those working remotely join via Skype). We closely monitor plan (or budget), forecast, and actual numbers.

3. Provide a stake in the outcome to all employees. We give employees a share of the success and the risk of failure. We teach people how the numbers influence each other and ultimately their own pocketbook.

Not *all* employees have influence over *all* the numbers, but they can see their impact on the bottom line. They behave as owners. One example involves a bonus plan we have related to top-line gross revenue. Although our seven production team members aren't salespeople, they have great influence over the sales numbers—if they don't make the chocolate, then we can't sell it. Production and sales are on the same page working toward the same goal, which isn't necessarily common in most organizations. But it's something we work at daily.

Why Do I Care? It's the Right Thing to Do.

It just so happens that Jack lives in my hometown and is my friend and mentor. When I was starting the business, I told him of my idea to use the open-book model with our new cocoa farmer suppliers. I proposed taking open book upstream and sharing profits with farmers and I asked if I could name this model after his book *A Stake in the Outcome*. He loved the idea and could see the benefits without further explanation from me. Jack's imprimatur in that three-minute conversation has been an anchor to our program, especially in times when I asked myself whether or not it matters to the farmers, to our customers, or even to our employees. He said something very simple to me, which he's repeated over the years: "Why do you care? It's the right thing to do." This open-book model of sharing with farmers is the right thing to do and that's why we do it.

The way it works is simple. On each origin trip, during which we discuss the coming year's crop and our next purchase, we bring a profit share to the farmers from our prior year's sales of chocolate made from those beans. We translate our financial statements into whatever language they need. We explain line by line how we arrived at the profit share calculation. Then we hand over cash in a farmer meeting with families present. We've been doing this since day one. It's easy to do in practice because we don't blend beans and we carefully monitor and record bean usage. It's easy to do in theory because we believe in it.

But our profit sharing isn't just for farmers; we engage our employees in Stake in the Outcome within the brick walls of our chocolate factory. Every Tuesday morning we have our huddle—a meeting involving all sixteen of the Askinosie Chocolate team members. Nearly everyone plays a part by sharing an update on his or her area of responsibility. We also review financial statements, discuss big projects, and talk about the company's current and forecasted condition. We analyze detailed comparisons of forecasts versus actual versus the plan.

Everyone is on the same page as to where the company is financially—and hopes to be—at any given time. Everyone feels ownership. We reward our team financially with bonuses (called "Mini Games") as we hit targets and perform better.

An Engaged Staff and Supply Chain Equals a Better Business

As far as I know, we are the only chocolate makers who are also the direct importers of cocoa beans in the United States. And we're the only chocolate makers in the United States directly trading on several continents and importing our own cocoa beans. This is not because we possess superpowers or have some secret information. It's because it's part of our business vocation. Don't get me wrong, it is cool being the "first and only," but we do it because we think it's the best way to practice business. Any organization can have happy employees, a gracious, action-oriented culture, and meaningful vendor and supplier relationships. All it takes is a little planning and a lot of tenacity. Intentionally and thoughtfully engaging with our partners in business, both internally and externally, pays dividends in more ways than one.

Direct Trade vs. Fair Trade: What Is the Difference?

First things first: what is direct trade? One of the best ways to describe it is to begin by saying what it isn't. Direct trade is not a certification by a third-party auditing body. It's not Fair Trade. It's not free trade. It's not a government-regulated phrase, which means that anyone can print it on a package and nobody will be arrested and charged if they're not actually doing it. People often say "free trade" when they mean Fair Trade. Free trade is an economic trade policy of commerce between countries without tariffs, duties, or restrictions imposed. We are not talking about free trade here, but we are going to take a little ride down the Fair Trade river.

I was first exposed to Fair Trade in 2005, coincidentally around the time I started the company. My daughter, Lawren, then fifteen, desperately wanted to go to the Austin City Limits Music Festival, so I took her (I took her out of school for it, too, because, after all, what is teenage rebellion if not skipping school to go to a music festival with your dad?). I've been taking her to concerts since she was seven; it's one of our "things." It was 108 degrees for three days in a row but that's another matter. Anyway, while we were watching Coldplay she told me about the tattoo that the lead singer, whose name escapes me but he was married to Gwyneth Paltrow, had on his hand supporting Fair Trade. Actually she said it was not a tattoo but probably a Sharpie drawing and really it was for an Oxfam campaign but whatever; the point is Lawren was the one to bring Fair Trade to my attention, as she often does with things like fashion, art, food, culture, and music. We talked that weekend about Fair Trade. Immediately I felt there was something not quite right about it, but I couldn't put my finger on what exactly.

Modern-day Fair Trade is a certification, represented by a seal or label on a product. The origins of the movement stem from the desire for fair treatment of farmers, and eventually handicraft makers, with the rise of alternative trade organizations (ATOs). The origins of Fair Trade are noble and in many cases were driven by faith-based groups. The global Fair Trade movement over the last sixty years has been responsible for, among other things, economic, social, and environmental advancements for small farmers the world over. Moreover, Fair Trade marketing has elevated consumer consciousness about the plight of small farmers (or artisans) who have poor working conditions and don't earn enough money for their crops (or goods).

Fair Trade: A Bumper Sticker, the Cost of Doing Business, or Both?

I never considered Fair Trade certification as a viable option for us for a variety of reasons. First, some critics of Fair Trade cocoa beans assert that farmers are not receiving the premium price that consumers pay for Fair Trade goods. From everything I have read in the last ten years, I think that's true. Second, there is a huge cost to farmers who want their small farms certified Fair Trade. I knew that the farmers we would be working with were smallholders, owning three to six acres, and loosely organized in small groups or co-ops. They could not afford this kind of certification. The Fair Trade system is not structured for companies like ours; it's better suited for big companies like Whole Foods or Starbucks.

In August 2011, we received an invitation from Whole Foods to visit its HQ in Austin to attend the "Whole Trade Summit" at the Intercontinental Hotel, as one of four chocolate companies in America. I was honored by the attention and immediately began daydreaming about the possible opportunities that would arise for our tiny business from this day-long workshop. As it turned out, the meeting, attended by cool brands from across the country, was a long pitch as to why we all needed to be third party certified. After a Whole Foods vice president's speech that afternoon I introduced myself to him, explained how tiny we were, and said that we could not afford these certifications and neither could the farmers. I also explained my concern that farmers were not seeing the Fair Trade premiums. He answered by suggesting that we explore a way for Whole Foods to help pay for the certification. I took his card, gave him mine, and it never went any further. At the end of that day, the chocolate makers had a smaller meeting with the global buyer, who told me that the retail chain would not be able to carry our product nationally if we didn't obtain one of those certifications. Today, we work with a few select Whole Foods stores around the country. Ultimately, we decided that we would rather not seek the certifications and not be carried nationally. Paying for Fair Trade certification was the cost of doing business with Whole Foods at a national level. As tempting as it was to think about Whole Foods helping pay for a certification, it was and is inconsistent with our views. We've decided to invest that money in something we think is better, which is direct trade. That's a real price we pay; and we're happy to do it.

THE COST OF FAIR TRADE

The premiums that buyers/importers like myself must pay in order to be Fair Trade certified are minuscule in comparison to the cocoa world market price. When I started looking into it in 2007, the buyer/importer premium was $150 per metric ton of cocoa beans (in 2011 it was raised to $200). That means even if the world market commodity price for cocoa was at $2,000 per ton, buyers like me were required to pay only the farmer Fair Trade premium of $150 per ton for the certification. Really? That's it? Yes, that's it. So for all the warm fuzzies that we shoppers might get in the chocolate aisle when we reach for a Fair Trade product (anything—doesn't have to be chocolate), we think we can feel good knowing that the higher price we are paying at the register goes to the farmer who worked so hard to bring the crop to market. Let's pretend for a minute that all of it goes to the actual farmers—spoiler alert, it does not—it's still not enough! We are, therefore, lulled into a sense of "feel good" or "my work here is done" as we put the product in our basket and continue through the store, due in large part to the hugely successful marketing efforts of the Fair Trade movement.

We are not Fair Trade certified because we've found what we think is a better way. Better for us, better for the farmers, that we think produces better-tasting chocolate in the end.

Direct Trade Means Better Products, Better Organizational Cultures, and Better Communities

Intelligentsia Coffee pioneered direct trade coffee. It's the *way* they buy coffee. I stumbled upon Intelligentsia in early 2007 and started a dialogue with Geoff Watts, the rock star of the coffee world, cofounder of Intelligentsia, and the man responsible for initiating the company's direct trade practices many years ago. When my factory was in its infancy and I was still devising our direct trade framework, he obliged me by giving me advice and taking time to answer some of my dumb questions. Full disclosure: Intelligentsia has become one of our largest customers in the last few years. We make a custom single-origin dark chocolate that they use in all their chocolate drinks. We also collaborate on a chocolate bar infused with their single-origin coffee. And they sell our chocolate bars in their coffee shops around the country. I started the relationship with Geoff not because I wanted them to buy our chocolate but because I needed expert assistance with some practical issues related to our cocoa buying practices. Over time our aligned philosophies created synergies that led to them becoming a customer.

This is how we define direct trade. I could devote an entire chapter to waxing poetic about what direct trade means to me. But our definition is pretty simple: direct trade is knowing and having a relationship with our cocoa farmers, who we refer to as our "farmer partners"—because that's what they are; we consider them partners in our business. For us, "knowing" and "having a relationship with" mean visiting our farmer partners at least once per year; spending time in their homes, meeting their kids, enjoying a meal with their family. In a word: kinship. We work with them on sustainable growing, postharvest techniques, fermentation, export, cocoa bean quality—the list goes on. It is business, after all; good business, in fact. Direct trade is about honoring our farmer partners. It's about working together in a spirit of mutuality, service, and respect. It's about keeping promises, showing up, and working together toward the goal of crafting the best chocolate possible.

Tenets of Direct Trade

Officially, there are important and practical components to the application of direct trade in our business—we have five tenets. First, the cocoa beans must be excellent in quality. Our farmer partners know we accept only premium beans, the definition of which is clearly outlined in our contracts with them and the creation of which we counsel them on. Inspection of the beans is one of the reasons why we visit them yearly. Second, there is financial and transactional transparency. We profit share with our farmer partners and open our books to them, in their language, each time we profit share, and they retain intimate knowledge of our business. Third, they—and we—practice ecological and economical sustainability. It's very important to us that our cocoa beans are grown and harvested using sustainable environmental practices such as pruning, intercropping, and shade growing. In some cases, we educate our farmer partners on these things when we begin working with them. Additionally, if they seek our counsel we will advise our farmer partners about smart investments of their profit share cash back into their business. This happens during the visioning process with farmers. Fourth, the farmers must practice socially sound business; that means no child or slave labor, and fair wages for laborers where applicable, as outlined in our contracts. Fifth, we visit our farmer partners at least once per year.

At your company you can define direct trade differently than we do, but you need to say what it means to your company, and most importantly you'd better do what you say. It's pretty simple, actually: if you're going to market to folks that your company does *X*, *Y*, and *Z*, you should do it. It may seem foolish for me to even say this, but I've seen too many companies write beautiful copy for their websites and social media that they don't actually follow through with in real life. If you're pulling at people's heartstrings to sell your product, do not misrepresent or embellish the truth. If your company is making "socially responsible" marketing claims, you have an enormous obligation to your customers because you're influencing people's emotions, you're asking them to invest their heart into what you're selling. You're building people's trust. Don't mess with your customers' trust, *especially* not to make a buck.

When I started my business, Jack Stack gave me a very simple warning that I've never forgotten: "You better be doing what you say you're doing." To prove his point, he told me the sad story of the world's leading socially responsible cosmetics company, based in the U.K., which sourced its ingredients from farmers around the world. He told me about the founder of the company, that she was a force for good in the world, and that it all came crashing down when it was discovered that she wasn't truthful about claims she'd made regarding sourcing and many other things. I say that it's sad because many of her company's stories of doing good were fabricated. It's sad because we trust and then things like this happen and it can cause us to be cynical the next time we hear a story of good.

Trust Me

This important story, and many others just like it, brings to mind Nobel Prize–winning economist Milton Friedman's contention that the duty of business is maximizing profits and shareholder value. That anything other than adherence to this doctrine would not be socially responsible. The corollary to this maxim, as framed by *New York Times* economics columnist Eduardo Porter: "You can trust a business that merely wants to turn a profit in a way that you cannot quite trust one that wants to change the world, too."[1] This philosophy has dominated the business world ever since, especially among larger companies. People rarely question it. But while there is nothing inherently wrong with this profit-driven model, we think you can do both: aim to be profitable and do good. I've said it before and I'll say it again: we can't do the good work we do unless we make great chocolate that people want to buy.

It's just like your mom taught you: do what you say you're going to do. Being deceptive about your company's social responsibility discredits the entire movement. It makes all of us look bad. People become cynical after they've been lied to, and I understand. Skeptics ask, "How can I believe what you're saying?" My answer: trust us. Our model is value driven. The model is proven over time; character reveals itself over time. Because we prioritize transparency, we owe our customers honesty and authenticity. We do all we can to verify what we say we do by sharing stories and pictures on our website and social media; connecting our farmer partners to our customers by featuring their names, faces, and stories on our packaging; releasing ten years of profit share data; and more.

Third-party certifications are one way to assuage consumers' lingering doubts over the authenticity of a company's claims, but we both know those only go so far. Those certifying bodies are flawed, too, and resting on them alone is letting ourselves off the hook too easily. The real key here is trust. Ultimately it's your choice and I can't force you to trust me. But trust is the foundation of every personal relationship, so why shouldn't it be the foundation of business relationships, too? If I take advantage of your trust, I am the one to blame. Then you stop purchasing my products and my business fails. I'm incentivized to maintain your trust; not only is being honest the right thing to do, it's

---

1   https://www.nytimes.com/2014/07/16/business/the-do-good-corporation.html.

in my best interest as well. This is how evolved societies operate and function at their highest level.

Direct Trade Doesn't Stop with Farmers

We also trade directly with our customers. We sell to folks in a little store at the front of our factory (which is open plan, so you can see almost our entire production process), online, and to retailers, chefs, and restaurants around the United States and Canada. We choose not to use distributors. We're in nearly one thousand specialty food shops, bakeries, coffee shops, department stores, boutiques, restaurants, and more, and we deal with each and every one of them directly. Did I mention we also have only a three-person sales team? We remove as many layers between us and people who enjoy our chocolate as possible. When the owners or staff of a store or bakery have something they want to ask they call us; if their order is incorrect they call us; when they have a great story to share, or piece of feedback, they call us. And we love it this way. We have customers who've been buying at our storefront for ten years. We know them by name. The same is true for our online shop. These relationships are so important to us that one of our employees is dedicated to thanking our customers in meaningful ways. We want connection. This is our fuel. It makes our business better and our chocolate better.

Mary Frances, an elderly woman from Michigan, routinely called us for about nine years with the same request: ten white chocolate pistachio bars. Pretty much everybody in the factory talked to her over the years, and we all knew about her. She didn't just call us to place an order, she called and gave us her kindness. She would chitchat with our staff and talk about her family. We never met her in person. We were connected, though. When she died recently, her husband sent us the obituary with a note to me that said, "She loved your chocolate and all of your staff." We sent her family a small magnolia tree on Mother's

Day with a note: "We have had the pleasure to call Mary Frances our best customer, but she was so much more than that. She nurtured and helped us grow, not only as a business but individually. She left a lasting impression on every generation of Askinosie team members and we are forever indebted to the kindness she shared with us." I call that direct trade; I call that kinship. Mary was our friend.

What we call direct trade on the retail level is what the business world calls the "direct to consumer" model. It is a freight train gaining speed by the day and companies across the globe are betting on this strategy for many reasons. Lower price to the customer, higher margins, speed to market, and more profit are chief among them. This sales channel is the best chance for a retail relationship between makers and those who enjoy the products they make. The cotton you use in those cool jeans has a backstory waiting to be told, but the department store is not able to tell the story like you can. What better way to honor your business vocation than by meeting people like Mary Frances, who care about what you do, as opposed to waiting to hear about her from a store that is also selling fifty other products just like yours—but not just like yours.

My wife Caron's grandfather was a butcher and owned a tiny grocery store in Olney, Texas (population 2,000), when she was a little girl. He knew nearly everyone in town, calling them by name when they came in the store. He had about 250 customers who loved him. They would run up a tab, settling up with him at the end of the month. He knew what cut of meat his customers liked. When children came to the store he instinctively knew what their mother had sent them for. Farmers brought eggs in and he gave them store credit. He made deliveries around town and people would leave their back door open for him. Customers often called just as he was on his way home for lunch (because they knew what time he left) and asked him to deliver a quart of milk on his way, and he gladly did. That little store supported his family of six and put four children through college.

Caron's grandfather had connection, relationships, and mutuality.

We can reclaim relationships like this by practicing direct trade with our customers. Remember, we don't need a million of them. We just need enough.

The Universal Truths of Direct Trade

My grandparents' small farm remains a major influence in my life. Their lives as farmers, neighbors, churchgoers, and grandparents over the years painted a deep and rich picture for me of what it is to be human. That spilled into my adult life, even after their deaths, so much so that when I think of farming I think of them. To me, and I know this is a naive thought, all farmers everywhere are like them: kind, hardworking, honest, giving, fair, and hospitable. This naïveté would prove to be both my creative savior and an occasional weak spot, from which I've learned a lot—more on this later.

At the very beginning of my journey, my first step was to find farmers growing excellent cocoa beans who we could trade with directly. This, itself, is a very challenging process, and it was even more difficult over a decade ago when I was first getting started. How did I find these farmers? Well, I had a little experience finding people, namely, witnesses who didn't want to be found and didn't want to talk to me. I've translated that skill into finding farmers. It's not complicated, but it's not easy. I research, dig, uncover, then do more research. Then I network and network until I find what I am looking for. In the first years it was: I know people who know people who know farmers. Now I know people who know farmers. That's how I find them, and the route to every farmer group we have worked with over the years has been different and in some cases very circuitous.

You may be wondering how direct trade can apply to your business model. The good news is there are endless possibilities! The fundamental notions behind the concept are applicable to nearly any organization, regardless of whether you're a manufacturer like we are. Our direct trade practices contain truths that are universally transferrable whether you operate a tech company or a hair salon.

1. **Quality**

Practicing direct trade improves the quality of your product or service. Do you remember the story of Mamma Mpoki from the beginning of this chapter? If not for our deep partnership with these farmers, our Tanzania chocolate bar would not have been awarded this honor (not to mention the countless other bits of praise and recognition it's received). The farmers also understand that better-quality beans means better-quality chocolate, and better-quality chocolate means more sales, and more sales means more profit share.

Our cocoa bean contracts have a long list of quality specifications. Direct trade gives us the chance to actually see with our own eyes the progress of those quality steps in the process of a *Theobroma cacao* tree eventually yielding a superb and flavorful cocoa bean. In other words, we can influence those steps and see them in person year after year. Direct trade produces better quality because it incentivizes better quality.

All the component parts of our direct trade practice when viewed in total make for a better product, better chocolate. Profit sharing with farmers, opening books, community development, working with local students—all these things are part of every chocolate bar we make.

Ari Weinzweig equates direct trade with "buying local," something that is central to the Zingerman's philosophy. The people at Zingerman's define "local" as having a relationship with the people they buy from and the people they sell to. Ari explains, "When you made cheese for your family, if you cared about them and about food then you had a high incentive to make it really good. Then when you made a little surplus, in the early nineteenth century, you started taking it to town to sell—you still had an incentive to make it good because most of the people you were selling to were people you knew in the town. But then they started pooling milk in the last half of the nineteenth century and there's twenty farms all in there together; you've been busting your ass to make great milk and your cousin doesn't and you're getting paid the same price. After a while, what's the point? When you have direct trade like Askinosie it just enhances everything. Quality wins out and it tastes better."[2] Ari says that their Reuben sandwich (and everything they make) tastes better because of who they are as a company, applying these principles every day. Does this sound familiar? It should because Ari is expressing the same message we are: relationships make for a better-quality product. When you know your customers— our direct trade-to-consumer model—you are simply more incentivized to do the absolute best you can. When you know your suppliers—in our case, cocoa farmers—they're incentivized to do the same. The result? An excellent product that is the combined efforts of many people having given their absolute all.

2. **Others' Vocation**

Suppliers, vendors, and growers are our partners. They know we value what they do. They see us when we visit, they feel our dedication, and they know we care, so they care, too. Although this supports our vocation, it's also an opportunity for us to help give life to *their* vocation and be part of it in whatever small or large way we can. Buying a thing with layers of distribution and brokers is fine and sometimes the only way,

---

2 Interview with Ari Weinzweig, January 8, 2017.

but it reduces the chance for connection—on both sides of the equation. The more layers, the more separation.

One of the most important aspects of an origin trip is chocolate tasting with the farmers. It's one way for them to know that we care about them and the beans they harvest for us. Let me tell you: it's not easy bringing chocolate to the Equator, given the challenge of heat and humidity and oftentimes lack of reliable power, but it's worth it. Tasting chocolate is imperative, not only because it's educational but because it's community building. It's our version of breaking bread. In some cases, the farmers and their families are as excited about tasting chocolate as they are about the profit share cash. When I visit them I bring chocolate made from their cocoa beans, but I also bring chocolate made from other origins' beans as well. Obviously it's fun to share chocolate with our farmer partners; after all, most of them never tasted dark chocolate (or in many cases *any* chocolate) before they began working with our company. When I announce it's time to taste, the size of the group seems to swell as children, passersby, and folks on the periphery saunter closer to the group. There's hushed tones and quiet excitement as everyone closes in and patiently waits for me (or Lawren—when she travels with me this is always one of her favorite activities) to hand them pieces. We want to honor the farmers' work by bringing them chocolate made with their beans and the smiles it brings to their faces reflects the hard work involved to make this flavor a reality. The farmers' appreciation for our trouble is never lost on me. In every case, the farmers and their families have the same universal response, which surprised me at first, and that is reverence. They have a sense of pride, which seems to hold them back from immediately plopping that square of chocolate straight into their mouths without thought.

But we don't haul chocolate across the world just for fun, we do it because it's very informative for the farmers. In addition to the chocolate, we bring roasted beans to give the farmers a sense of the flavor profile we are expecting from their beans. This is serious business, but the farmers always say how it helps them to see the full picture—how their work fits into the larger framework of "great chocolate." So we do this each and every year, in hopes that recognition of our flavor and aroma become second nature. It's best when we can actually roast beans with farmers over an open fire so together we can experience the process of heat and aroma. We also bring fully packaged chocolate bars with us so we can show the farmers our packaging, which highlights their work: the lead farmer's face is on the front, along with the name of the city or village, and their story on the back. And of course we always bring enough chocolate to give them to enjoy or share later after we've gone home.

We don't know the personal vocation of most of our farmer partners, but we know their business vocation is to produce premium cocoa beans. We are proud to contribute toward their goals by honoring their vocation with our work of turning their beans into a great bar of chocolate. It is an honor and a privilege for us.

Helping others find their vocation doesn't apply to just the supply chain. If you own an insurance company, it's feasible for you to meet your customers from time to time and get to know them. What I am proposing here is something more. If your insurance agents really get to know their clients, and even their clients' families, it's possible for your company to help those clients see their vision come to life. Or take the example of an advertising firm. Sure, it helps people with logos and branding but what if its mission included helping clients uncover their "true selves" and discover their vocation? Sometimes this means additional work for companies (and I bet it feels worth it!), but not always. Companies can sometimes help facilitate others' vocation simply by doing the work they normally do, and introducing empathy and kinship into their relationships.

3. **Price**

Direct trade permits us the chance to influence price paid to the supplier. The closer I can get to the people who made or grew the thing, the better chance I have of putting more money directly in their pocket. The fashion industry, for example, has in recent years made efforts to shorten the supply chain, getting closer to the source of production, for this very reason. The caveat to this is that when you get closer to the source, it's harder to push back on price if your partner is living in poverty.

Over the last ten years, since we started, we've paid farmers 47 percent more than the "farm gate" price. This is what they would otherwise have received at the front gate of their farm if they sold on the open market. In the Philippines, we took it a step further and trained the members of the cocoa cooperative how to become a legal exporter so they could do it themselves and keep more money. The first year we bought beans in Tanzania, in 2010, we paid the farmers a very high price. It was so high that other multinational chocolate companies complained to the local government that "Askinosie is paying too much" to the farmers. During contract discussions the following year, in 2011, the farmers told us the price for cocoa beans in all of Tanzania was elevated because of our little purchase in 2010! That, my friends, is influencing price.

Influencing price has long-term effects as well. I've been working with our lead farmer partner, Vitaliano, in Ecuador over eleven years, longer than any other farmer. He was born on his small farm and has worked with cocoa his entire life. He and his wife have six sons and a daughter. His daughter is a doctor in Ecuador and they paid all of her school from the profits of this small farm! Four of his sons farm with him and are passionate about their work. Vitaliano's father died when he was seventeen. He told me his father's dying request was: "Please don't sell this land because it is the hope for life." Vitaliano says that it's proven to be true. He tells me that our work together all of these years has helped him keep his farm, make it better, and provide for his family. Direct trade with Vitaliano has given us a chance to influence the price we pay and in turn the profit he makes from his farm—his "hope for life."

If your vocation is to make an impact on the people you work with, then raising the price you pay the poorest part of the supply chain is substantial. Here's what I mean: If we charged $1 extra for a chocolate bar, the impact on the customer may be 0.001 percent of their paycheck. On the other hand, if we raise the price we pay farmers from $2 to $3 per kilo of beans, that's a 50 percent increase in their income. That extra money doesn't buy a movie night or a self-storage unit for extra furniture. It buys education, medicine, and a new roof. (See appendix A for details of what income cocoa farmers *actually* make.)

In your business, is there something you source that may not dramatically affect your margin if the price goes up? For example, if you run a bakery and source pecans, you might consider the direct trade methods we outline here, which would have a direct impact on the price you pay to the producer. Perhaps an increase in price would not hurt you but would help the growers significantly.

4. Traceability

Direct trade allows us to better trace an item and know its history; we can rely on the information when it can be traced all the way back to its source. Likewise, we can share the story with our customers, who can trust what we say. The practical aspect of traceability is that it fits snugly with its cousin, transparency. Tracing a product permits us to share more information with even greater detail with anyone and everyone.

Product traceability also gives customers reassurance. Skeptics have something they can point to and say, "This company is doing what it says it's doing." For example, customers can rely on the fact that their traceable milk was not mixed with all the other milk, the substandard milk, Ari was talking about previously. Direct trade practices give additional reassurance for customers because representatives of the company go to the source over and over to see everything with their own eyes. When I travel to meet with farmers there is a higher level of credibility than if we relied on brokers or someone else to verify that the beans we're buying are the beans they are shipping, that they're of excellent quality and harvested according to our contract specifications. This is an important issue, because it's not uncommon for substandard cocoa beans to be combined with higher-quality beans at export warehouses. Sometimes this is by accident and other times not. Direct trade substantially reduces this possibility.

Sharing your adventures, successes, and even trials and tribulations is an important part of the process. It connects the circle; you've done these things, now go spread the word. Your customers want to hear your stories, and as we discussed earlier you owe them your (honest) stories if you're directly trading. This applies to any business acting on its vocation.

People want authenticity. Share yours and then bask in the rewards, and even in the criticism, when it comes—it's an opportunity to engage in real discussion.

Geoff Watts says:

> There is another aspect to our enjoyment of coffee, beyond its flavor attributes. Knowing where it came from, who produced it, and what sorts of substantive details lie behind the unique flavor profile and character of a coffee can jack up the amount of pleasure we can get from drinking it. There's a world of flavor nuance to explore and understand, and direct trade opens a doorway to that.[3]

We've spent years connecting our farmers to our customers—both retail and wholesale—fostering mutual appreciation and understanding. It makes our business better and our chocolate better to create a discussion and even a community around good chocolate and ethical sourcing practices. People want to know where their food comes from, and we show them. We show them, as mentioned, on the package of the actual chocolate bar, by introducing them to the face and name of the lead farmer who harvested the cocoa beans. We show them on our website, with detailed accounts and pictures of each trip to origin I've made since 2005. We share our story on our social media accounts, creating a hashtag for each origin so folks can follow along with my journey while I'm there. They can see the farmers who grow the beans, their children, their homes, the cocoa pods on the trees in their backyard, the place where we hold our meetings when I'm in their village, the food that we share and oftentimes prepare together, and so on.

---

3   E-mail to author, January 12, 2017.

At first, sharing our story felt weird. I was worried it would seem like bragging. Then I realized that if you're authentic, and you share your failures along with your accomplishments, and you do it all with a sense of humor, then people will connect with that. We've learned that our customers want to hear from us, even the not-so-pretty stuff. The more transparent we are, the better our relationships are, across the board.

I would be remiss if I didn't mention this very important point: when sharing the story of the folks you're working with in developing countries, do so with humility and respect. Let's officially establish one thing, if it wasn't already clear: in almost every origin, we work in remote village communities with extreme poverty. Everywhere you turn there is a spectacle of destitution and "third world" scenes to gawk at, if that's what you're looking for. We try to look instead for the joy, for the people, for the kinship; these aren't hard to find. When telling these stories to your customers, make sure to emphasize the dignities and joys of the producers—not just the pain and suffering. Likewise, take care not to be exploitive with your images. We all know the saying "a picture's worth a thousand words." So we choose our images—and the words accompanying those images—with extreme care, as much care as we give to our cocoa beans. We aim always to share these stories from this place of humility, appreciation, and kinship. These are people, real people just like us, with complex lives and stories, beyond the straw hut they may be living in. Would you want someone strolling into some part of your life that isn't picture-perfect and publish the image in a catalog that implies, "Feel sorry for this person. Buy this product that supports them!"? Far too often, companies with a "socially responsible" mission fail at this task, reducing the poor, the disenfranchised, and all too often, Africans, to a pitiful image—or worse yet, a would-be pitiful image if it weren't for the "Great White Savior" costarring in it. Don't be intimidated by how to share the story; just share it, all of it. We'll all be so much better for it.

We don't see ourselves as the "Great White Savior," and as a company we are eager and careful not to portray ourselves as such. We are not "saving" the people with whom we work in developing countries. First and foremost, we're simply doing the right thing by treating folks in every aspect of our business fairly. Second, we're just practicing good business. And of course we're also building kinship from positions of mutuality. If anything, our farmer partners are saving us. I learn more from them about life, community, family, friendship, loyalty, and trust than I could ever hope to impart. This also reflects what we teach our Chocolate University students. I teach the farmers some about cocoa beans, sure. We try to educate about business and finance and improving yields. But they give me so much more than that.

Traceability is important, but it's also not always easily reduced to a sound bite. And that's okay.

5. **Relationship Sustainability**

Direct trade enhances the sustainability of the buyer-seller relationship by setting the stage for the long term. Our efforts create a foundation for our suppliers, which will be helpful not only for other Askinosie employees, both present and future, but also for other individuals and companies that might want to do business with these farmers. Individual relationships develop between people quickly and deeply due to the history of the organizational connections. We have found that practically everyone we bring with us to meet our farmer partners in Tanzania are immediately treated as "friends of the family."

The contact is not corporate entity to entity, it's people. Those people, our agents, pave the way for others to join in the relationship much quicker than without these practices. For example, Lawren and others from our company have been with me on trips visiting farmers and inspecting the crop for the coming year's shipment. What if I want to slow down my travel schedule someday? It will be relatively easy because the road has been paved for someone else to visit and be welcomed with open arms.

Maybe you're a fashion designer with a small brand and you want to produce your clothes in America, and work directly with your textile manufacturer. For example, if you're designing jeans, there are a handful of denim mills in the United States that you can develop a relationship with. Maybe it's a family mill, and you get to know one another as individuals. This opening of your hearts to each other, and seeing each other as human beings in kinship, will allow for a long and flourishing relationship between your companies, even as individuals come and go.

In order to build a sustainable long-term relationship framework I need to spend time in kinship with people. I can't just sit in my hotel room and only show up for business meetings.

Over the years I've stayed in farmers' homes to learn, to have fun, and most of all to deepen my relationship with them. One of the most meaningful experiences of any origin trip was an unplanned overnight stay in the home of one of the farmers we do business with in San Jose del Tambo, Ecuador. It turned out that the hotels in the village (probably not the kind you're thinking of) were overbooked. After I had my main meeting with the farmers I asked, "Might any of you have a place for me to sleep tonight?" The president of the cocoa association and her husband immediately said that I would stay with them. I had never done this before. She had our little group over for a dinner of homemade maize tortillas with cheese and soy coffee. I admit I was a little nervous to sleep there; it was way outside my comfort zone. But I was also excited, and hoped that it would deepen our relationship.

My host promised to make us traditional Ecuadorian hot chocolate if I woke up at 5:00 a.m. to help her with the process. Five a.m. came pretty early, since it seemed like the roosters started in around 1:30 a.m. and did not let up all night long. I began by helping her roast cocoa beans on her stovetop, then we shelled them, reheated the beans a little to soften them, and took turns grinding them in a *molino*, which produced the paste. After she added a touch of cinnamon and panela, she heated it with fresh cows' milk and we had ourselves some "made from the bean" traditional hot chocolate. What an experience! Since then, I've felt a closeness with this family that would not have happened otherwise. I have no doubt that anyone from my company would be as welcome in their home as I was that night.

I have since spent the night in the home of a farmer in Tanzania and it was also moving in a way that I will never forget. I often contemplate the reasons that people in such poverty, who have so little, would want to share what they have with the likes of me. I call this "radical hospitality" and I have not experienced it this intensely anywhere in the world. I am humbled not by the conditions in which my friends live, but by the attitude which allows them to thrive.

You can probably imagine how our Chocolate University students feel when they meet our farmer partners for the first time. The existing relationship I have with the farmers sets the stage for this "radical hospitality." One of our recent students, Emma, said it best: "The greatest impact of the trip was the hospitality of the farmers. They do not have much, but they welcomed us into their homes, fed us tea, eggs, and bread every day, and treated us like old friends even though we had never met before."

Are these relationship-building experiences possible without direct trade? Of course. However, direct trade generates more opportunities. My aim—and your aim—should be to create relationships that transcend "business," to create a path for others to come alongside you and benefit from the groundwork you've laid.

6. Your Vocation

Direct trade practices might lead to your business vocation. If you have an existing supply chain in place then working with suppliers puts you face-to-face with human beings who just might need you, and help lead you to your vocation. You might need them, too, for connection, mutuality, and kinship afforded by direct trade. I would have never known about the water conditions (which prompted us to drill a well) in the remote Tanzanian village where we buy cocoa beans if we'd never traveled there. I would have never known about the malnutrition at the school in the Philippines if I'd stayed at home.

If you're a buyer for a men's clothing store, what would happen if you visited some of the factories that produce the shirts you sell? It's possible you will find people who give you joy. If you own a restaurant and visit the farms that grow your produce you might meet people you want to get to know even better.

As of now, I've made thirty-two origin trips visiting with farmers over the past eleven years. Traveling to these distant places and meeting people is something that I love. I don't mind delayed flights, sitting at an airport in Manila overnight until my flight leaves at 5:00 a.m., the unfamiliar food, the challenge of it all. In other words, I love the process that leads to direct trade. Most importantly, though, the physical act of going to the place has opened my eyes, ears, and heart to humanity. Direct trade is part of our vocation, but the preparation that precedes it has enriched our vocation. What I am saying is that if you're unsure of your business vocation but take the risk of going to the place and meeting the people, then you will assuredly discover new aspects of your vocation.

7. **Solving Problems**

Not only can we learn more about our communities by implementing direct trade principles, but we might have the chance to partner in the solution of some very difficult social problems. Entrepreneurs are by definition "problem solvers"; we're already predisposed to uncovering solutions to vexing problems in our communities. The principle of empathy behind direct trade equips us to contribute to solutions to problems of basic human needs: food, shelter, medical care, education, and kinship. We have a duty to help where we can and direct trade will put the human condition in front of us and challenge us to not look away. It's about developing and fostering compassion, the most important virtue anyone can learn.

This would be easy to gloss over. It's important to consider that your vocation can be a catalyst for change. The chronic undernutrition rate for rural students in Tanzania is 45 percent. The undernutrition rate at Mwaya Secondary School, where we began our sustainable lunch program nearly four years ago, is 0.7 percent.[4] Our program has made a difference. Additionally, there have been zero abortion deaths since we

---

4   Convoy of Hope 2016 Mwaya Impact Report, Daudi Msseemmaa, Africa/Asia field director.

started this program. I just returned from the Philippines, where I was meeting with farmers and checking in on our new Baguio school lunch program. The principal told me that there were ninety-five children suffering from malnourishment nine months ago when we started the project, and now there are only four. She predicts that by the end of the school year there will be zero.

The problems your company might be able to address could show up anywhere. Take the example of the fashion designer working with the family-run denim mill. As the head of the clothing company, maybe you want to help the mill tell its story, as a way to promote its products. If you learn more about the people at the mill then you will no doubt learn about the methods they employ to source the cotton. You might come face-to-face with social and environmental issues troubling the industry. The closer you connect to the source, the greater your likelihood of uncovering things you can't turn away from. For instance, there are lots of pesticides used in cotton farming. Plus it's a thirsty crop, and uses tons of water. And there's an issue with the use of forced labor.

Here is the amazing thing about this: You don't have to be the owner of the fashion company or even a leading executive; maybe you're a buyer. Your entrepreneurial spirit gives you the drive to find out more, in order to consider the human concerns surrounding the cotton product you're selling. This quest generates in you a desire to bring this story back to the leaders of your company and persuade them to listen, take action, and make this work part of the company vocation.

8. **Sharing Profits**

Practicing direct trade will give you the opportunity to share profits with others in your supply chain. Our profit-sharing system with farmers, using open-book management, is dependent on direct trade; we would not know the farmers to share with if we used another method to source the beans! This reinforces transparent business practices. These ideas are all manifestations of transparency. Using direct trade and open-book ideas together we show the farmers (translated into their language) our numbers: revenue, expenses, and net income related to their beans and our overall company financial performance. The application of this idea could work in any business with integral supply chain actors. You can profit share with whomever you think appropriate. There's no law that says it's limited to employees.

I agree with Geoff Watts, who thinks that direct trade financial incentives influence quality. "Once the trade relationship is re-wired, coffee gets better in a hurry. Because there is real economic incentive to plant and produce more delicious coffees, and because the direct collaboration enables dialogue around both quality im-provement strategies and taste outcomes, the pathway to better tasting coffees becomes clear."[5]

When we profit share with farmers we have the opportunity to facilitate the visioning process for their small business. As an aside, we never tell the farmers what to do with the money. That is up to them to use as they see fit. However, when they ask us for assistance, the visioning process provides the farmers with hope and a plan. They then come up with great ideas of what to do with the cash they receive.

I remember walking alone on the county road in front of our house before I started my chocolate factory, thinking about where I could get cocoa beans and what the farmers must be like. I pondered the poverty of the farmers and what

---

5   E-mail to author, January 12, 2017.

ways my new business might interact with them. I didn't hear an audible voice, but I might as well have, because it was clear to me from the get-go that we should share profits as well as our financial statements. There was never any question or analysis or meeting about this; it was what I was going to do.

We have been buying beans from Vitaliano in Ecuador for many years. He sells his excess beans to a medium-sized industrial chocolate company. That company has indirectly observed us sharing profits on bean purchases there for ten years. Recently, we learned that the company is planning a profit share program with its farmer members, all one thousand of them. That is impact and it makes us proud.

How might a medium-sized company manage to share profits with a thousand individual farmers? There are two basic components of profit sharing. First, the company's leaders need to explain to the profit share distributees how they arrived at the share amount. This has to do with transparency and open-book management. It generates a great deal of goodwill if the farmers understand how the share was calculated and actually see the numbers. Second, the company must find a way to actually give the money to the recipients. That's not as easy as it sounds. In the case of one thousand farmers the company will want to distribute this at either one large meeting or a series of three or four smaller regional meetings. It's important that the farmers see each other receiving the money. The profit share must be out in the open so the entire group can see what's happening, in order to avoid any suspicion of corruption. In some cases it will be with a board of directors. The point is, profits can't be shared in front of an informal select group, or just one person. It's about transparency. As the saying goes, "sunshine is a powerful disinfectant."

9. Risks

At some point, something will go wrong in the direct trade process. While successful, the model is not immune to the occasional failure. We assume greater risks when we trade directly than if we used a broker (which we haven't). It's not easy to mitigate all financial risk, but we have learned how to protect ourselves from it pretty well. Understand that if you buy or source from a supplier outside the United States, then you bear great risk if you pay up front for the commodity like we do. There's no recourse. What am I going to do? Sue a farmer in the Philippines? I don't think so. Therefore, it's important in any direct trade scenario to plan for possible costly obstacles.

What can go wrong when practicing direct trade? Everything! I mentioned earlier how my general trust in farmers has sometimes caused me problems. I have several fairly harrowing stories to illustrate this point, but here are a few of the highlights.

Venezuela, or, as I Like to Call It, "The Place Where I Lost $25,000"

In 2006, right before our factory opened, and right after securing my first shipment of cocoa beans, from Ecuador, I traveled to Venezuela to source more beans. I had a missionary friend who introduced me to a man named Pastor Javier there. The pastor guided us all over the countryside, introducing us to farmers, who showed us their cocoa and their postharvest practices. After days of this we settled on partnering with one very small group. We spent a full day negotiating with them through their leader, Diego, and finally settled on quantity and price. I also explained our profit-sharing system. We shared a dinner together of freshly killed and cooked chicken and yucca on his small front porch. The next morning we received a frantic message from Pastor Javier that he wanted to meet us before we went back to Caracas. When we met, he said that God had told him during prayer late that night that we should not trust or do business with Diego and his group. The pastor assured us that he knew what we wanted and that I could send the money to him and he would handle the beans for us.

When I got back home I contacted the pastor and he said he was putting together my purchase of beans and that he needed the money to pay the farmers. Now, I am a lawyer and the following statement will cause many to lose confidence in my brainpower: I wired Pastor Javier the money for the beans, in all about $25,000. I also wired him money for Diego to build a drying pad. And I wired the pastor money to help him with the house he was building. That was in July 2006. One month of promises turned into three months, which turned into too many to count. No beans and no refund. I finally had to involve my missionary friend again, who drove many miles to meet with the pastor and the farmer who had our money. When he arrived he found the money had all been spent. I am no longer waiting for beans or money, as I heard the news last year of Diego's death from cancer. My disappointment has waned over the years. I was never too bitter about it, because I also blamed myself for being so foolish.

Tenende, or, as I Like to Call It, "The Place Where Our Farmer Partners Took Their Profit Share Money and Began a Coca-Cola Distribution Business"

When we first sourced Tanzania cocoa beans, we bought the crop from Tenende, a village that had no improved water source. We specifically sought a farmer group led by women, which we found. We worked to build partnerships in the community and together we achieved many successes in education, nutrition, access to water, and girls' empowerment. I attended church services and shared meals with farmers and others in the group. I visited one farmer's mud huts once and she tearfully explained that her children had no beds, so I personally bought mattresses for them.

We purchased beans from this farmer group in Tenende for three consecutive years. We helped them open a bank account in Tanzania so they could be paid directly. Our profit-sharing model helped these cocoa farming partners to diversify their business. Here's the rough part of the story: in 2013 they decided to convert their cocoa bean warehouse into the Tenende village's Coca-Cola depot. That's right, Coke. They would not have the cocoa beans for us. We were devastated. The first resulting emotion for me was one of sadness and disappointment. What about *kujengana* (Swahili for "build each other up")? How could this be, after all of the connection and partnership on important issues?

Well, *kujengana* for us meant renewed focus on sustainability of the programs we had in place in that community, specifically the school, Mwaya, where we've spent several years investing in sustainable lunch programs, electricity installation, and educational programs. We would not abandon them simply because they had abandoned the cocoa business. This was and is personal. During our visits there we meet with parents, teachers, students, and government leaders to talk about how the programs can operate without outside help, but our commitments have remained in place despite what happened. We doubled down in our dedication to the school regardless of its distance to our new cocoa bean village.

Community development is messy enough in my own neighborhood, but it's exponentially messy in the developing world. It's a good reminder for me because I know that we must constantly evaluate our definition of success, and success here was them selling Coke, and us finding this new outstanding farmer group whose beans are superb and who we're thrilled to develop a long relationship with, and it's also led by a woman. *Kujengana* continues.

EXERCISES

....

1. Carefully examine your supply chain and list the top five critical vendors and suppliers you rely on.

2. If you deployed your own version of direct trade practices with any of the groups, people, or companies on that list, would the quality of your product or service improve?

3. How would you define direct trade in your business? What are the guiding principles?

4. The universal truths of direct trade are: improved quality, support to our partner suppliers' vocation, price influence, traceability, sustainability, deepening our own business vocation, business solutions applied to social problems, profit sharing and transparency, and risk.

    List the truths from this list that apply to your business, or that relate to a project you want to implement.

    What can you add to this list that is not universal but applies only to your industry or business?

    What are the risks if your business embarks on the direct trade path? Are there financial risks that can be mitigated? How?

5. Do you know anyone in your industry who is currently successfully applying direct trade principles? Who is your Geoff Watts? Ask that person if he or she can coach you on a rollout of your direct trade program. It's very important to have specific questions ready.

6. Do you think your customers would care if you applied direct trade ideas in your supply chain? And if so, why would they care; and if not, would you do it anyway?

7. If your company started a profit-sharing plan with someone in your supply chain, who would it be? How would you make a profit-sharing plan work?

8. How can you communicate and work more directly with your customers?

CHAPTER 5

....

Don't Scale, Reverse Scale

"Small Business" Is Not Small Business

"Shawn, this is such a great program. I love it. What would you need to scale this up? How big could you scale it? How much money do you need to scale it up fast?"

I've had that conversation on more than one occasion, including once with an executive of Unilever. At first, the executive's interest took me off guard. I was proud that someone so important, well funded, and connected would be interested in what our little company was doing. I felt validated in my work. I daydreamed about how great it would be if we scaled some of our projects exponentially—like Chocolate University engaging students all over the world, or A Product of Change school lunch program feeding kids throughout sub-Saharan Africa. She said that if I could figure out a way to scale *and* tell the story, then the TED people might be interested in me for a talk. As she asked me these questions I stopped taking notes, sat up straight in my chair, and pressed the phone to my ear to make certain I could hear every single word; our chocolate factory can be loud. I was both flustered (which rarely happens) and excited. In order to buy a few moments of time and pull articulate answers from my brain I repeated the questions back to her. Leaning forward at my desk, I offered, "Sure, we can scale these programs . . ." not really knowing what I was talking about. My brain began firing at lightning speed, though, and I came up with a plan of scale, on the spot. "We can do this and we can do that," and "All I need is the right partner and enough money." "How much money?" she asked. Great question, I thought. She said she could introduce me to the right people when I delivered more details about scale. She also mentioned that the World Bank might like me to give a speech about our model and programs. I had visions of the TED intro music in my head, standing on the TED stage saying really wise and witty things about scaling this, that, or the other to change the world. To hard-charging, make-it-happen entrepreneurs, that is an intoxicating dream.

When I hung up the phone I was embarrassed at myself because I'd gotten caught up in her enthusiasm, and when I came back down to earth, I was too nervous to tell her the truth: that we don't really want to scale, that we are doing about all we can do, that we are a tiny chocolate company, not a gargantuan multinational corporation.

The allure of notoriety and recognition is strong. After all, what's so wrong with scaling projects designed for the social good? More people benefit from scale! And more is better, right?! But I demurred. I eventually gained the courage to disclose to her that we are not in the position to scale and it's not my calling. To my surprise, she understood and appreciated my stance. Over the last four years this Unilever executive has been one of our company's greatest advocates, tirelessly introducing me to many people who have helped us immensely.

Less than a year later I was tempted yet again to scale, this time from Target. Todd Waterbury, vice president of marketing and chief creative officer, invited me to speak at the company's headquarters in

Minneapolis for the quarterly marketing huddle. Lawren and I put on a chocolate tasting for the team of two hundred and told the story of Askinosie Chocolate. We left feeling inspired and affirmed. A few months later, they asked if we would be interested in making a chocolate bar for their Made to Matter collection. Target execs said they wanted to learn more about how our factory of sixteen people manages to do what we do and see if there were any applications for their company. Target wanted to learn from *us?* We were honored. And after a year of planning we did make a chocolate bar just for them, eighty-five thousand to be exact. (Target, through us, purchased the same beans from our farmer group in southwestern Tanzania, at the same premium we pay!) I remember one special meeting; Todd was listening intently to what I was saying and turned to another VP and said, "Their company is about reverse scale, touching one person at a time, and keeping their soul." I absorbed that and never forgot about it.

Target was great to work with, but a series of executive layoffs changed the picture for us. The new people said that since we couldn't make enough (more) bars for them and lower the price (below what we sell to others for), it would not be a good fit for another order. I completely understood their thinking. But what Todd gave us was much more than a great sale. In his simple description of our business to his colleague, he reaffirmed the value of human scale. It's ironic that an executive from one of the biggest stores on the planet would help me articulate a guiding principle of our business model.

Think Small to Solve More Problems

Why did I hesitate scaling and pursuing the TED stage? And why was leaving behind the next Target order easier for me? Because the essential question that I come back to is: what do I want? I know in my heart that it's not viral video recognition and 1 million social media followers. My personal vocation is to follow a path and develop relationships that continually allow me the opportunity to have my heart transformed and become my true self. My business vocation? Not to necessarily get bigger, but to get better at staying small.

Most everyone is asking the same question about any entrepreneurial idea: will it scale? Investors want to know for obvious reasons. Your chamber of commerce people will ask because they wonder about more jobs. People who like and support your vocation will ask because they care about you and your success. They equate scale with more. More money, more followers, more customers, more people you can affect and help. Here's the big question, though: if we scale can we remain true to ourselves?

I propose we invert the original question and ask, "Does the idea have *reverse* scale possibilities?" Let's turn the scale pyramid upside down. What if we consider the impact a good idea might have on *one* person? Or ask, "How will it change me?" This approach gives us a greater likelihood of transformation because of the personal connection with another human being in need, which over the long term is the greatest scale of all. Why? Because we produce more change when we change ourselves. And a more compassionate world will solve big problems and produce joy at the same time.

Deep, Not Wide: The Real Impact Begins

Leaders should deploy reverse scale in order to achieve depth, not breadth, of vocational projects. There are too many ideas a thousand miles wide and one inch deep. And their impact? Well, it's not very sustainable. Of course, scaling in and of itself is not inherently bad. We want to scale antimalarial meds, postdisaster food distribution, and vaccines. In fact, we are obligated to scale when it comes to issues of imminent human suffering. Beyond that, though, we have to be careful that we are scaling for the right reasons and not simply because we can. It's tough because the world nudges—or strong-arms—you to scale.

The danger is that with scale we risk losing some of the benefits of our vocation. We tend to lose ourselves. We lose connection and kinship under the intense focus of scale for scale's sake. And so it is important to know that there is honor and validity in ideas that are not scalable.

Scale is proportional to the size of your company. Target has 341,000 employees, so the measure of scale for Target will be different than for us. Between 2010 and 2015, Target gave $1 billion to education programs here in the United States and around the world. Philanthropy is not new to this one-hundred-year-old company. This giving initiative to local schools was true community engagement, but the program ended in 2015 (it has refocused its giving on health and wellness initiatives). My note to Target: please keep giving to education! Target never intended for this program to be anything other than an inch deep and a million miles wide, and it benefited tens of thousands of students across the world. In addition, the company could consider programs that reverse scale, benefit the community, and engage its own employees at lower levels than its chief corporate social responsibility officer, in order to transform more hearts within and outside of the organization. Target, one of the largest consumer goods retailers in the world, is not too big to implement a reverse scale program.

The benefits of reverse scale are supremely sustainable and transformative if enough people take their own ideas (especially the small ones) and just do them. If there were more small companies practicing reverse scale, we might not have to think about scale as much! There's a misconception that in order for an idea to be worthy, it must be "big." People stop themselves from pursuing excellent projects they've dreamed up because they mistakenly think, "I'm just one person with this small idea. I can't really create any valuable change or impact." If you've had that thought, you're wrong. No matter how small your idea, you will influence someone. And you, yourself, will be altered. More transformed people translates into sustainable impact and change.

As mentioned earlier in the book, the Catholic theologian Jean Vanier founded L'Arche, a group of communities for people with intellectual disabilities. Seemingly destined to follow in his father's footsteps, for a time Vanier commanded an aircraft carrier in the Royal Navy. Eventually, though, he left the military in pursuit of a spiritual calling. He earned a Ph.D. on Aristotle's ideas on ethics from the Institut Catholique de Paris in 1962 and then taught philosophy. In 1964, while visiting Paris, he learned of the plight of thousands of institutionalized developmentally challenged people and invited two of the men he'd met, Philippe and Raphael, to live with him in a house in Trosly-Breuil, France. He "sent out a call for people of good will to help him."[1] Many young people responded and eventually the house transformed into a community of people with disabilities and those caring for them. Jean says that Philippe and Raphael did not care very much about what he could do or what they could learn from him. They needed "my heart and my being." They wanted a friend. Today there are 147 L'Arche communities around the world. Jean, now eighty-eight, continues to live in a home in Trosly-Breuil to this day.

His messages of love, service, hope, and compassion inspired my own ideas about vocation. Although he doesn't call it this, Vanier's message echoes that of reverse scale:

> We have to remind ourselves constantly that we are not saviors. We are simply a tiny sign, among thousands of others, that love is possible, that the world is not condemned to a struggle between oppressors and oppressed, that class and racial warfare is not inevitable.[2]

---

1 http://www.jean-vanier.org/en/the_man/biography/short_biography.

2 Vanier, J. 1989. *Community & Growth*. London: Darton, Longman and Todd, 312. Retrieved from http://www.goodreads.com/quotes/254319-we-have-to-remind-ourselves -constantly-that-we-are-not.

I cling to this sentiment especially when I feel discouraged. I return again to the reality that I only need to do one small thing and hope that others will be encouraged by our example.

Pema Chödrön, Buddhist nun and author, repeats Jean Vanier's conclusion that Philippe and Raphael needed his heart and being when she says, "Compassion is not a relationship between the healer and the wounded. It's a relationship between equals. . . . Compassion becomes real when we recognize our shared humanity." This is the way to kinship and real impact.[3]

Continue Serving and Stay Tethered to Your Vocation

Rather than only taking big ideas and using binoculars, we also need to take big ideas and use a microscope.

Is it possible to start by connecting with one person? It is in the smallness and particularity that we find relationships and experience pain, challenges, and hope. "More" and "bigger" will always be enticing because we think achieving them means we can breathe easier in our businesses and rest on the laurels of our good works. It's also appealing to scale because bigger numbers fill our egos and give us a cleaner story to tell. It's great for marketing! It simply sounds better if we tell a story of reaching X number of people with Y thing. But if we scale, then it's likely we will need to start delegating tasks to others, who will then have the connections with people that we once had. We will be supervising, managing, writing checks, and generally insulated from the joys and sorrows of human connection. We risk building insular layers around ourselves and we can end up being service providers helping service recipients.

---

3 Chödrön, P. 2007. *The Places That Scare You: A Guide to Fearlessness in Difficult Times.* Boulder: Shambhala, 74.

Earlier I said that Father Greg Boyle's book introduced me to the idea of kinship. He also introduced me to a deeper meaning of the word "mutuality" than I'd ever considered. He has spent the past thirty years working with and living among gang members in Los Angeles. His daily experience with kindness, hope, heartache, and even death has deepened his humility about roles and labels where humanity is concerned. His wise guidance is worthy of emulation:

> I'm not the great healer and that gang member over there is in need of my exquisite healing. The truth is, it's mutual and that, as much as we are called to bridge the distance that exists between us, we have to acknowledge that there's a distance even in service. You know, a service provider, you're the service recipient and you want to bridge even that so that you can get to this place of utter mutuality.[4]

Mutuality is the key to staying on course. I don't want to delegate that to another employee, unless it's so they can experience mutuality, too. It is the job of our chief kinship officer to integrate kinship throughout our company and plug our team members into projects we're doing that they're excited about, but I'm still just as involved in those projects now as I was on day one.

I've said that the final step to finding your vocation is to continue opening your heart to a need with no expectation of profit or benefit. This is the practice that keeps us tethered to our vocation day by day. We never finally arrive at our true self destination, wash our hands of the process, and call it good. Becoming our true self is like grabbing fog. It is, however, momentary glimpses of our true self that affirm us to our very core. These flashes are available to us when we open our

---

4 https://onbeing.org/programs/greg-boyle-the-calling-of-delight-gangs-service -andkinship/.

hearts to a place of service again and again. The reverse scale environment is well suited for these moments to rise up around us. If we keep our hearts open, and don't look for validation, then we can hear and see what we might otherwise miss.

Waking Up to Your True Self

Reverse scale could also be called human scale. It's these human connections, which allow us to be transformed, that have ripple effects in myriad ways. I'm grateful for the opportunity to build these relationships because it renews my focus on my vocation and points me back toward my true self. I know that change begins with me, and that when we invest in each other, magical things happen. Below are four such examples.

Visioning with Empowered Girls

Upendo, Maria, and Saraphiner

Visioning work is something I'm very comfortable with. I've facilitated visioning workshops for companies, churches, and entrepreneurs. Nonetheless, it felt like a curveball when Lawren and I got a request for help with visioning while visiting our farmer partners in Tanzania. The Mababu village school where we'd started an Empowered Girls club asked if Lawren and I could lead an afternoon vision workshop. The next day. For two hundred middle school girls. I'm always up for a challenge, but I gulped at the request, telling our host that we weren't exactly qualified to do this work. I politely explained that we'd never led any students in this process, let alone two hundred middle school girls in rural Tanzania. Our hosts insisted, so I nervously agreed.

Lawren shared my trepidation. We were in over our heads. She thought we should prepare for the likelihood that the girls would struggle with articulating their future because, living in such poverty, they have to focus most of their energy on meeting their daily needs. So I did what I normally do when I'm stuck: I called on Ari. As you know by now, Ari has been one of my mentors for nearly a decade. I texted him from Mababu and succinctly laid out the problem at hand. He replied that I should seek volunteers and ask the question: "Have you ever imagined something that would happen in the future and then it happened as you imagined it?" Simple, yet brilliant. This is something we've all experienced, or so I thought.

The next afternoon, girls crowded together for the workshop in a small open-air classroom at their school, which lies at the base of Livingston Mountain. We could hear the girls singing loudly in Swahili as we approached. The founder of Empowered Girls, our translator and guide, Kellen Msseemmaa, warmly greeted us and gave us the floor. Silence. Hundreds of shining eyes stared at us, curious about what we had to say. Lawren spoke first. She enthusiastically explained why we were there and who we were, and she introduced the concept of visioning. She is really good at communicating with people who may have different backgrounds and experiences than her. Partly, it's because she is a great listener. Then it was my turn. Still nervous, I stood up and honestly wasn't sure where I would begin.

I followed Ari's suggestion and asked for two volunteers. Upendo and Maria each raised their hands and walked to the front of the class while the other girls laughed and gently teased them. The three of us faced the rest of the class and I asked them both the question: "Have you ever imagined something that would happen in the future and then it happened as you imagined it?" Kellen translated and the girls were quiet. I should note that their names are saturated with meaning: Upendo means "love" in Swahili and Maria, well, you can probably guess her namesake is Mother Mary. I repeated the question and they both averted their eyes. I asked Kellen if my question was clear. Yes, she said, they both understood. I asked Maria if she could share first. . . . Silence. I began to panic, thinking I had started something that I might not be able to finish. Then, breaking the low murmur of her friends' giggles, she looked up and said that she had really never imagined anything in the future. She looked down again, turned to Kellen, and asked if I could come back to her. I felt short of breath. "Of course!" I offered. I felt such a shock of sadness that I almost couldn't stand up. Lawren had been right. I kept it together, telling myself to buck up and that this was not about me. I repeated the question, this time directed at Upendo. She responded, "Yes, I wanted to get a book because I wanted to read. I got the book and then read it." *Yes!* I yelled on the inside, but in reality I smiled widely and thanked her for a great example.

I wondered if I should follow up with Maria. I didn't want to put her on the spot, and I was nervous I'd make her feel bad. At that moment, I just wished I could give her a big hug. I repeated the question to her. She had thought of something, she said. She held her head up, looked ahead, and said, "I imagined that I was going to fetch some water," and she did do it. Her vision was to take a bath to feel clean. For a brief moment, I thought I might cry. A bath. Even today, I can't really explain what I felt there in the front of that hot classroom standing next to Upendo and Maria. The best I can say is that we dramatically and forcefully switched roles. I became the student and they were the teachers. Not just any teachers but wise, tall, strong, and powerful. In that moment, they took my breath away. I felt joy and gratitude. This is what kinship and mutuality look like. This is reverse scale in action. Lawren characterized it best: "Vision is hope plus a plan."

Once Upendo and Maria gave their examples, everything came to life. The other girls related to them, which opened up a lot of discussion. They asked us a bunch of questions, things that I know they would never have asked if Upendo and Maria hadn't shared their visions. They asked me what my greatest challenges were, what happened to me in school, and what my vision was. I began to truly appreciate "It's not about the chocolate, it's about the chocolate," and I understood what a powerful tool visioning can be.

After this experience, I couldn't leave this idea alone of teaching visioning to students. Upon returning to the States, and after talking further with Ari and our group, we decided that our next Chocolate University class would facilitate a written vision plan for four hundred middle students at Mababu village. Upendo and Maria continued to teach me from afar. Once we selected our new class, we set up a rigorous schedule to teach our local high school students how to facilitate visioning and plan how we were going to make it all happen. Our chief kinship officer and I modified Ari's visioning process. First we taught our students how to write their own vision of greatness for themselves. Then we trained them how to teach other students how to do this. Then we took our group of students over to Pipkin Middle School (a Chocolate University affiliate school), blocks from my factory, and our students facilitated written vision plans for the entire eighth grade. Our Pipkin faculty sponsor, Julia, said it was the most rewarding day in her fifteen-year teaching career. We translated the entire process into Swahili after making cultural adjustments. Feeling buoyed by our success, we prepared our students for the same process but with middle school students in remote Tanzania.

One year later—to the month—I was back together with Upendo and Maria. I thought it would be a good idea to see if they could both speak to all of their fellow students in the introduction before we began. I am not sure what happened in that year, but they were different young ladies in so many ways. I give much of the credit to the Empowered Girls program at the school. Upendo gave a rousing speech with the confidence of a presidential candidate. Needless to say, the experience wasn't easy, but it was memorable, successful, and powerful. We continue to follow up and work with each student on their visions for the future.

We recently hired our first Askinosie Chocolate Tanzania field representative, a young woman named Saraphiner—and her first job was to follow up with the school kids on the visioning process. Saraphiner is

Tanzanian and a recent graduate of the University of Dar es Salaam. She moved to Mababu village for this job. She interfaces with our farmer partners and facilitates our community development projects, often working directly with students in the empowerment programs. One of our favorite things about hiring Saraphiner was that she herself is a graduate of one of the Empowered Girls clubs.

We don't need to hire one hundred Saraphiners in order to live our vocation and we couldn't if we wanted to. Jean Vanier was once asked about a statement he made that L'Arche is "not a solution but a sign" and he replied: "You see, once I was speaking to a man in a big city in the United States. He said, 'Give me the formula and I'll create 300 L'Arches in the next two years.' I said, 'It doesn't work like that. It's a transmission of a vision and it's counter culture. But that's OK."[5] I'd like to think that Askinosie Chocolate is not a solution but a sign, a little lamp.

Our company has now facilitated the visioning process for hundreds of students in the United States and Tanzania, and we plan to continue with it. To think that it all began because of two young women, Upendo and Maria; these two hearts. They allowed me to glimpse my true self, to live out my personal vocation, and to give life to my business vocation.

ASKINOSIE CHOCOLATE TOUCHSTONE: TANZANIA FIELD REPRESENTATIVE, SARAPHINER URIO

As our relationship with our cocoa bean origin community in Tanzania deepened, it became clear that we needed someone there "on the ground." I'm there at least once per year, but we needed someone to be in constant communication with our farmer partners, to manage

---

5 http://www.onbeing.org/programs/jean-vanier-the-wisdom-of-tenderness/.

our sustainable lunch program, to operate the Empowered Girls and Enlightened Boys clubs, and to keep our team up to speed on all of the developments and progress. We knew we wanted to hire a Tanzanian. Then Lawren and I thought: wouldn't it be amazing if we could hire a graduate of Empowered Girls? So we did. Saraphiner represents our company by maintaining the strong relationships we have in the village, and she Skypes with us weekly to share updates. When we bring students to Tanzania, she will act as our "host"—translating, scheduling, and helping to organize our activities. It has been a unique experience, not without some challenges. But it's been endlessly rewarding, for us and also for the people of the Mababu community, who love Saraphiner.

When Things Come Full Circle

Elizabeth

Our Chocolate University high school program is very competitive. It's open to local juniors and seniors. For our last trip, we had about eighty applicants for fourteen positions. Eight of the positions were full scholarship and the remaining six were private pay. The cost is about $4,000 per student and the private-pay students can afford it—their parents are cardiologists or venture capitalists. Our scholarship students are no less meritorious, but in all cases very poor. To give you a sense of the caliber of student that we attract, one of our scholarship students from our class of 2012 is currently finishing at Yale University on a full scholarship.

A couple of years ago, I was reviewing the applicant essays and one in particular really stood out. This young woman mentioned that for a few years she'd lived at the homeless shelter that was a block from our factory. She'd participated in our elementary and middle school

Chocolate University programs. She also described visiting our factory with her little brother during her middle school years and said that we gave her chocolate samples to try and treated her like she was somebody. I had never met her. What struck me was that the people who worked for me didn't judge her by the clothes she wore, or the fact that she was alone with her little brother, or that she didn't arrive in a Mercedes. The people who work for me treated her like a human being.

Liz has given me permission to share this story and use her name. When I read her essay, I realized in that moment that we, as a company, had established kinship with her. We were a little sign of what is possible with that one heart. I realized that my business could fail tomorrow, but that we were a success. What Liz said about us might be the highest praise that we've ever received, above all awards, all honors, all press because it means that, at least for her, we lived our vocation and mission. And, yes, we selected her to be part of our Chocolate University class and she traveled to Tanzania with us in 2014.

The Warrior Bracelet

Mr. Livingston

I've spent more than a decade traveling to far-flung corners of the globe to visit farmers, pay them directly, share profits with them, and connect with their communities where we can. I have done this because I like it. And also because it's our business vocation. I like traveling long distances and meeting with farmers. I also go because it's one way in which I can honor my grandparents. Yet even after all those trips and miles, I would sometimes wonder if it mattered to farmers we work with. Did they care? In my most uncertain moments, usually when things were tough, I would worry about that. That all changed one evening a couple of years ago in Tanzania.

Every year on the last night of our trip, we host a celebration for the Mababu village farmers on the beach of Lake Nyasa. We help them cook all day long for this fun gathering. They roast a goat and always prepare usipa for me because they know I love those little crunchy fried fish, eaten whole. A couple of years ago, the party was like any other party with our farmer friends. At one point during the party Mr. Livingston, married to Mamma Mpoki (who is the chair of the Mababu Cooperative and pictured on the front of our Tanzania chocolate bar), took me aside and said he had something for me. He's an elder of the village, and someone I'd known for a while at that point. He handed me what looked like a very old bracelet. He explained that it was a tribal warrior wristband, passed down from his father, who'd received it from his grandfather. It was beautiful. Heavy and worn. It was a defensive tool, used, long ago, to block a club or other heavy weapon. Mr. Livingston handed it to me and said he wanted me to have it as a symbol of our friendship. I am guessing it was probably his most treasured item.

It's one of the most meaningful gifts I've ever received. I don't mean from farmers, I mean from anyone, ever. I was speechless, humbled, and floored. It was another moment of a glimpse of my true self. Expressions of gratitude were not enough and seemed almost hollow. That wristband is sitting two feet from me as I write this. I look at it nearly every day and think of its meaning.

The guessing is over. I know that I matter to Mr. Livingston and the feeling is mutual. He is my friend. The following summer when I visited, I gave Mr. Livingston my grandfather's silver pocket watch, which I've cherished since his death thirty years ago.

The day after I gave him the watch, we had just concluded the profit-sharing meeting in the farmers' newly constructed building in Mababu village (part of their vision, no less!). I was walking with our small group of students, winding our way on the trail to Mr. Livingston's house to show everyone his farm. Mr. Livingston came up beside me and took my right hand in his, and we walked together. I'll admit, I was a bit uncomfortable at first; this is not as common in our culture as it is in Tanzania and elsewhere around the world. I could feel forty years of farming calluses as we walked. After a few seconds, I eased into it and realized, this is what it's all about.

We Are Happy to Be Together

The trip from Springfield, Missouri, to Mababu, Tanzania, is about fifty-five hours door to door. We spend a lot of time preparing our students for the rigors of the journey. Many have never been outside of Missouri, much less on a plane. I explain that we will take an overnight flight to London and if we spend any time at all outside of the airport, they must watch for cars going the other way than they're used to. Then another overnight flight to Nairobi. I tell them that at this point, they will know they're not in Springfield anymore; that their senses will be engaged in a totally new experience. Then we will fly to Dar es Salaam (my least favorite airport in the world, for the record) to get on a puddle jumper across Tanzania to Mbeya, and travel in a large dilapidated vehicle called a "coaster" for about four hours to the place where we will stay near our farmer partners. I tell the students that by the time we reach Mbeya they will think that we've landed on another planet. They are always inevitably exhausted but eager to take it all in. The sights and sounds are new; even the smell is not comparable to anything in Springfield.

As a side note, I should insert here how I take our travel preparation to another level. It's taken me a while to develop the confidence to approach this as directly and bluntly as I do. We've been traveling to this place with local high school students since 2010. We've always had hands-on projects for our students. When we interview student candidates for our program they all have the same answer to the question: "Why do you want to be part of this program?" They humbly and innocently say, "I want to help the people of Africa." These students are all overachievers with 5.0 GPAs, involved in every club, volunteering in their spare moments, all aiming to go to great colleges. In the beginning of our program I was too unsure of myself to correct that noble notion of "helping" the people of Africa. Now once our students are selected, I dispel that idea very quickly.

At our first orientation meeting, with parents present, I say to our superstar students,

> Yes, we will drill water wells as we have in the past, we will bring textbooks to schools that have none, we will bring electricity to the school, we will work on nutrition, we will raise money to build classrooms, and work with Empowered Girls, but your "job," students, is not any of these things. It is not your job to "help" the people of Tanzania. Your job is to receive. Your job is to let your heart be transformed. And that is much more difficult than raising $15,000 for a water well.

We drill this into our students over many months so they are primed and ready by the time they land on Tanzanian soil.

Back to my story. We all fall into our beds that first night, wake up to a nice breakfast, get in the coaster, and drive to Mwaya Secondary School, our Chocolate University partner school not far from where we buy cocoa beans. We have had a long relationship with this school of about one thousand students. They know me and my company because I've been visiting for years and bringing students. On one particular recent trip the roads were markedly more washed out than normal; the area had had a difficult rainy season a few weeks prior. Our coaster kicked up dust and rocks as we all bump-bump-bumped along toward a grassy clearing where Mwaya sits. We rounded a corner and I saw the school in the distance, but this time I noticed that the students were running and skipping down the long path from the school to greet us on the road.

You know this scene. It's the one where you are visiting your cousins for Thanksgiving and after an eight-hour drive, as you pull into the driveway, they come out of their house to greet you. You can tell that they are genuinely excited to see you and you think, "They really *do* want to see us!" and it makes you warm inside. Or, you've been the one to step out of your house to embrace your friends who've made a long journey to see you, before they even make it to your door. Multiply that times one thousand. Our coaster stopped on the road and as our students began stepping off the bus, one by one we were engulfed in a sea of students clapping and singing in English, "We are happy, we are happy to be together," over and over. I was the last one to depart the coaster and I took a quick thirty-second video. I stopped videoing, though, because I wanted to be part of it, wanted to be engulfed, and so I did. There was not a dry eye among our group. Not me, the seasoned traveler, or Lawren, nobody. We were all simply overwhelmed with hospitality that we couldn't handle. Most people have never experienced a blanket of hospitality; it can be difficult to process. Plain and simple, that much love, warmth, and joy makes you emotional.

I don't often keep photos or videos on my phone, but I keep that one and play it often as I contemplate the experience. At first I thought, This is what heaven will be like. I will step off of a coaster and be overcome by the welcome. As I've reflected on it more, though, I've come to believe that it was, in fact, heaven. For a brief moment, I experienced a tiny sliver of heaven.

Recently, one of our students wrote me a nice thank-you note and she concluded by saying, "I realized that I need Tanzania a lot more than Tanzania needs me."

This Little Lamp of Mine

This is the essence of reverse scale. This kinship would not have been possible for me if I had delegated this task to another person in my company. If I had decided I was too busy to lead a small group of Springfield, Missouri, high school students to meet farmers in Tanzania, I would have missed this transformative experience.

I return again and again to the unfolding nature of our business vocation and permit myself the chance to experience who I really am. If we stay home, unwilling to roll up our sleeves, then we reduce the likelihood of mutuality and kinship to near zero. This is why the path to our vocation never ends. It's like a flower continually blooming before our eyes, unfolding new possibilities for us to experience something beyond joy. All the while, I resist the temptation to scale it up. I remind myself that I don't want to change the world. I can't change the world. My guide on this point is, once again, Jean Vanier, who said:

> If I change, and I seek to be more open to people and less frightened of relationship, if I begin to see what is beautiful within them, if I recognize also that there's brokenness because I'm also broken, and that's OK, then there's something that begins to happen. But it's so counterculture but that doesn't matter. What has happened, what I sense for the future of our poor little world, with all its ecological difficulties and financial difficulties, that maybe the big thing that's going to happen is that little lights of love will spread over the country. Little places where people love each other, and welcome the poor and the broken. Where each other, we give to each other their gifts, and have these little, little places. And that the world is, you know, we'll never hit the headlines but we'll be creating these little lamps. And if there are sufficient number of little, little lamps in each village or each city and parts of the city, well then the glow will be a little bit greater.[6]

My goal is to be a little lamp myself, and for our company to be one, too. That is what I want. The words of Gandhi reverberate here: in losing ourselves to the service of others, we find ourselves.

---

6 https://www.onbeing.org/programs/jean-vanier-the-wisdom-of-tenderness/.

It's tough to find yourself when you're distanced from others. Scale demands that every single person in the chain focus on what's next and on finding someone to do the thing that's now "below" them in order to move themselves up. The ends are supposed to justify the means. Scaling up posits that there's a plan to get somewhere, someday, where we will finally be able to breathe and enjoy and smell and touch and learn. Anything less than that and you will lose the race for scale, because someone else is more focused than you.

Reverse scale, on the other hand, says, "This is it." Today, right here, right now. This bean, this bar, this student, this village, this employee, this customer. *That* is what I do, that is what I work for, in the present moment. I can't pass the buck to a future me, a me with more scale. All I can do is own right here and right now. And there's a lot of power in that.

EXERCISES

1. Can you think of a time in your business when you've said to yourself or your partners, "It will not get any better than this. This is something I will always remember and treasure even if the business closes and fails?" What was it about that thing that caused you to feel that way? Can you live it as a daily practice?

2. Thinking of the story of Upendo and Maria, can you recall a time when you were ambivalent about a task you were asked to do but you did it anyway and something great happened? Can you think of a time when something supposedly little turned into something big and unexpected?

3. Thinking of the story of Elizabeth, can you describe the impact that your business has had on one person? Can you think of one instance when your everyday work touched someone?

4. Have you ever received a gift that you think you might not have deserved? I posed this question recently at Pipkin Middle School during a hot cocoa holiday event. Hands went up and I called on one young man. I asked him to explain, if he was willing. He said that his parents bought him an Xbox and he felt as though he didn't deserve it. I asked him how it made him feel. He looked down and replied, "Sad." I agreed with him and acknowledged how the feeling of sadness seems natural when we receive something we might not deserve. I nudged him a little bit further and asked why. "Because my parents could have used that money to buy food for our family." I thanked him for his candor and used that as a launching pad to tell my Mr. Livingston story. Have you encountered something like this in your work life? What did you do about it?

5. Have you ever been overcome with emotion because of kinship derived from your work? What led to that experience? Can it be repeated?

6. After reflecting on Vanier's "little lamp" metaphor, how can your company be a "little lamp"? Is that enough, or, put another way, is that small enough?

CHAPTER 6

....

A Rule of Life

Ancient Monasticism for Modern Business

Father Cyprian is tall and thin, with no facial hair and a close haircut that he gives himself. In his movie, he would be played by James Cromwell. His face is almost expressionless, but somehow warm. His voice during readings from the pulpit is quiet and his words slow, and sometimes they run together, almost like a song. In conversation, though, he is measured, deliberate, and loud.

For the last sixteen years, I've had the pleasure of going for walks with Father Cyprian in the wilderness surrounding Assumption Abbey, the Trappist community in Missouri with which I'm affiliated. We walk in all weathers and seasons on the desolate roads cutting through the national forest, talking about God, life, work, and prayer—and developing my Rule of Life, which has affected every part of my life including my business.

I have a picture of Father Cyprian on one of our first walks: he's standing in the forest with a smile, wearing his robes, but he's also wearing this distressed jean jacket layered over a hooded sweatshirt and black worn-in Converse sneakers. He looks like the most hip monk on the planet. Lawren has always said it's one of her favorite pictures of all time and thinks it should be a Converse ad. Father Cyprian laughed when she told him that.

He entered monastic life in 1950. Think about this: he's been chanting the Psalms every day for the last sixty-seven years. I think it's done something to his face and skin. I am not saying that chanting psalms is good skin care, but I am suggesting that singing the entire Psalter (there are 150) every two weeks for over six decades has affected the muscles in his face in the best way. Cyprian is relaxed and every ounce of him oozes peace, calm, and tranquillity. It's truly visible. Of course I can't prove it, but I also think that his sixty-seven years of seeking the face of God has, in a sense, put light in his own face.

In my adult life I have attended at least six different churches. I haven't always been a stable churchgoer, but the abbey has been my center point all of these years. There are times when I find myself yearning to go there, not so much as an escape from my life but into the peace and rest that the holy place brings me. It's hard to describe the feeling of being pulled to a place. It's as if I am walking through my life a little bit chilled and I need to warm up by the fire. When I come back I feel like I am home. The scent of incense hangs in the air. The building smells a good kind of musty and I like that. Another thing that strikes me each time I return to the abbey is how much it stays the same. As I attend the first prayer service of my retreat, I notice that each monk is in the same place he was the last time I was there. My life has rolled on with ups and downs; meanwhile they were here chanting, praying, working, and reading and might not have even left the grounds. They stand still while I keep turning. That is the abbey for me.

Trappist monks have a long and deep relationship with work. Over the centuries, they have become known for the high-quality products they make—they are famous for their beer, cheese, incense, and many other products. Trappists choose work that is conducive to prayer. Thirty years ago, the monks of Assumption Abby made concrete blocks to support their contemplative existence. Now they make fruitcake. There are two kinds of people in this world: those who love fruitcake and those who don't. I love it. Theirs is an especially good recipe, with a strong pedigree: it was given to them by the former chef of the Duke and Duchess of Windsor. The famous Assumption Abbey fruitcakes are sought after around the country. Most are sold to Williams-Sonoma. This commitment to crafting an excellent product has inspired my own approach to chocolate making through the years.

Freedom in Rules

This chapter focuses solely on our interior lives. It's related to your personal vocation and doesn't directly address your business. But not only have I found immeasurable personal riches in tending to my soul—or my mind, if you prefer—it has also formed the basis of my business vocation. The goings-on in my head and my heart, and the efforts I've made to find peace and fortitude and resilience, have yielded many fruits in my professional life. I know the same will be true for you.

For me, creating and sustaining a Rule of Life has proven essential to my personal and business vocation. Anyone can have such a Rule; monk habit not required. And in this chapter, I'll share how to create your own. If you've been bruised and tattered by religion, you might relate to my winding path of faith and purpose—and how my Rule has provided necessary focus to my life and my company. Or if you're uncertain about whether or what you believe, a Rule of Life does not have to involve God. But it does have to be about something bigger than yourself. Maybe that is loving humankind, or serving other people. Maybe it's social justice, world peace, or the search for truth.

Whatever it is, it must be at the center of your belief system, however loosely defined that system may be. And while it's true a person need not have a Rule to live out their calling or lead a meaningful life, creating one can bring clarity to your vocation, which can lead to greater fulfillment.

My Rule of Life (which appears in its entirety in appendix C) is based loosely on the Rule of Benedict. Now, remember: I am a lawyer. So what's the first thing I did? I researched the best way to write my Rule. Of course I found very little on the subject, and eventually I dug deeper. I knew that the bones of the Rule would be based on the radical balance of prayer, work, study, and recreation. It's true that writing my Rule was tedious, but the process itself was like a test—a nanoparticle of the real experience of a new monk—or in my case, living out my Rule.

I think of the Rule as the nucleus of a series of concentric circles—it is our heart, our true self, and the point from which everything in our life flows. It is why we live and what we live for. Those circles surrounding the Rule, like ripples from dropping a pebble in a pond, provide daily context and color. These are our vocations. If we are living out a Rule of Life, which in turn informs our vocation, then how can we not lead a meaningful life?

As a human being and as an entrepreneur I need a center point. I need it for guidance; I need it as a source of character; I need it because I don't want my business to take its place at the center. I need a center point for creativity; I need it to remind me how small I am; I need it as my home base that I can continually return to.

Some of us are aimlessly adrift in an infinite void, not knowing our vocation for years, if ever. But everyone has a vocation, usually several. Creating a Rule has anchored me and given my vocations the context and direction they always needed. If you're looking to create a spiritual framework for your personal and business vocations, I'll explain how I did that, using my own, personal Rule of Life as an example.

Arriving at Assumption Abbey

My dad's tragic death from lung cancer when I was fourteen was a life-defining, traumatic event. I didn't know it at the time, but it would eventually lead me to my vocation—and to Assumption Abbey.

At age thirty-nine, I had successfully concluded my third, and what would be my final, murder trial. This one took its toll on me emotionally. Famed criminal defense lawyer Gerry Spence once said that with each case a little spoonful of your soul is scooped out and never returned. I had heard that, and now I knew it to be true.

Around this time, a photographer friend of mine told me about his assignment to shoot this famous fruitcake for the *Los Angeles Times* at Assumption Abbey. Yes, that abbey. On a whim, I called the monastery and spoke to a monk named Father Theodore and shared the story about my father spending his final night there. I asked if, by chance, they had guest books dating back to when my father died. Amazingly, they did. He mailed me a nice note, along with a photocopy of the page where my father signed the guest book on the weekend he died; the names of his church friends who had joined him there were beneath his. I put the page flat on my desk and ran my fingers over his signature, knowing it was the last time he'd signed his name. Transfixed on each letter of his name I choked back tears as I saw him standing at the guest book. It was as if I thought something magic was going to happen as I touched the page. And it did. Father Theodore invited me to visit the monastery for a retreat. Though I was apprehensive, I decided to make an appointment at the guesthouse for a retreat at Assumption Abbey.

I had never been on a retreat and, to be honest, I didn't really know what it meant. I only knew that it was something my father had experienced the weekend he died. Retreat sounded like something that you didn't want to do: as in hiding, turning around and going the other direction, or retreating in war.

As I was driving to the abbey that day in February 2001, my mind was full, my thoughts scattered. Once I reached Douglas County the trees started to change. It was beautiful.

Here are some journal entries from my first visit to Assumption Abbey:

February 1, 2001: *I am now back in my room, which is about the size of my bathroom at home. One twin bed, one desk with a lamp, a chair, and a small shared bathroom. I have no cell phone, pager, PalmPilot, or laptop!* [For those of you born after 1990, a pager and a PalmPilot can be found on eBay.] *The monks call their rooms a "cell." I just returned from my first prayer service and it's one of the most serene moments I can recall. The monks sang or chanted the Psalms and it was beautiful. They lined either side of the chapel and the whole service was chanting. Dinner is celery soup, potato salad, homemade bread, and a cookie. Not too bad.*

February 2, 2001: *I woke up at 3:30 a.m. for Vigils (the first prayer service of the day) and was sort of bleary-eyed but I made it. No angels visited me in the night (thankfully) but I am much more comfortable and now maybe I am ready to listen to God. The service was simple and a great way to start the day. The lights were on and then off again. I spent most of my time meditating on the candle at the altar. I thought I saw a butterfly in the glow of the flame.*

3:30 p.m.: *I met Father Cyprian this afternoon for an hour and a half. He has been a priest and Trappist Monk here at the Abbey since 1952. I explained as briefly as possible my story. Father Cyprian listened to me and it was so nice. My friend Tobias Meeker said that the "spirit is palpable here" and how true that is. Father Theodore said he had a theory about that, "the people who come here bring it with them." I talked to Father Cyprian about my issues generally and my fear of death particularly. Cyprian is about the age my dad would be. I have never been in the presence of a wiser person than this man. He radiates humility and wisdom.*

I have returned every year since that first retreat sixteen years ago. I usually visit once or twice per year; sometimes more, sometimes less. I have kept a journal of every visit and record nearly every detail of my conversations with Father Cyprian. We walk and talk and I can barely keep up with him. He's eighty-six now. He is more than a friend and mentor. The best way to describe it is that he is my spiritual director.

Becoming a Family Brother

During one of our walks about three years ago down State Road OO, Father Cyprian introduced me to the idea of becoming a family brother. I was immediately intrigued. He explained that it would be a way for me to deepen my relationship with the abbey without becoming a full-fledged monk. Cyprian's first question, though, was about my wife and what she would think of the idea. This is his theme with me: what does Caron think? We decided I should begin by speaking with her.

Did you know that one does not need to be Catholic in order to be a family brother? I am still an Episcopalian, though I have adopted some Catholic practices, like using a rosary, and praying the Hail Mary. Nor do lay people have to be male in order to associate with monasteries. Assumption Abbey has women associates who are similar to family brothers. The Benedictines have oblate programs for women who want to deepen their spiritual lives, as do most other orders of the Catholic Church and many are ecumenical. Oblates are similar to family brothers. While I am not as familiar with them, I am aware of some Buddhist communities that accept both men and women as lay brothers and sisters. For example, Thich Nhat Hanh's Plum Village in France has a program for longer-term female guests.

After discussing the idea with Caron, I was even more excited and I pressed Father Cyprian about whether it would be possible given my hectic international travel schedule.

This was where I got ahead of myself. I didn't listen to him; I only heard what I wanted to hear. I have a tendency to do this. He was abbot during this time, so I assumed that he could "make it happen" and that since he'd known me for so long he could simply deem me a family brother (or something like that). While this experience has humbled me, as many things have over the years, in that moment I had this entitled inkling that even if there were some pesky rules or procedures to follow, they would make an exception for me. Looking back, I'm embarrassed. None of that mattered, though, because by the time I was able to dig into this concept of family brotherhood, Father Cyprian was no longer the abbot. He suggested that I speak to the monk in charge of the program. Baffled and dismayed, I connected with Father Paul. Father Paul has been the family brother director for many years. In May 2013 he sent me the program document, which states, "A Family Brother, while not a candidate to become a Solemn Professed monk, is desirous of sharing more fully in our Cistercian spirituality, values, and way of life." When Father Paul sent me this document, I knew immediately this was what I wanted, needed, and longed to be part of.

When I talked with Father Paul about the specific requirements of becoming a family brother, he asked me to come for a week and stay inside the cloister—not the guesthouse—and live the life of a monk. Then we would continue the discussion. I explained to him that I run a chocolate factory, which meant I frequently traveled internationally and I might not be able to visit the monastery as often or stay as long as they would prefer. I asked if they could possibly make an exception given my schedule.

I was really concerned about what he would say in response. I thought if I added some details about helping people when I traveled, like our sustainable lunch programs, it might buy me some leverage. As I look back on that bargaining with the monks for special treatment I am not very proud of myself. Father Paul was gracious with me and said that we could talk about that later during my visit.

Brother Francis is the guestmaster and residential family brother director. Communicating with him and Father Paul about my Rule lasted almost a year. An e-mail in June 2013 turned into a string of back-and-forth messages until March 2014. This was not the kind of communication that I had grown accustomed to, which was instantaneous-response e-mail. At first this felt more like communicating with my Amish friends who built my home. Over the ten months, I slowly began to understand that our communication was not simply a lesson in patience and humility but in rhythm. The monks live by flow and rhythm. So I went with their flow.

In June 2013, Father Paul wrote to tell me that the amount of time I proposed for my first visit as a family brother candidate was not sufficient, that it would need to be longer. I would be traveling to Honduras and Africa for work that summer in addition to a number of domestic trips to see customers. Father Paul said, "We think it best, then, to cancel your July 27–28 scheduled visit until you can find your way clear for at least five days in which to taste our life as a first step. I hope you understand our conclusion that to be part of [Assumption Abbey] entails a more in-depth immersion in our life." When I read that, I was disappointed, but also incredulous. Or perhaps indignant.

I sent Father Paul some of our chocolate to try. He let me know that he really is not a dark chocolate kind of guy. Great news. But he grew to understand and appreciate our business vocation. He also grew to understand me, which was evident when he wrote, "It will be important while you are here to focus on a contemplative orientation, trying for a deepening of 'being' as a complement to your abundant 'doing.' We can talk about what balance will look like in your life."

What a simple but profound statement. "Being" instead of "doing." I only wish someone had suggested this to me in my twenties. He underscored this in a later message to me just before my visit in October. "As for what I would hope while you are with us, try to move into the full rhythm of the hours, spend time in deepening your discipline of contemplation, and I will want you to write out the typical daily and weekly schedule as you now live it, with beginning thought about changes that might arise in your attempt to be more monastic in your life and living."

I began working on my Rule immediately.

The Candidate Visit

When I arrived for my first candidate visit in October, Brother Francis told me my room number and when I asked about a key he peered over his book with a smile and said, "The doors don't lock." Oh, yes. Of course. What did I think? That a monk was going to swipe my coffee mug or Bible? I had been in certain parts of the cloister before, like the refectory and offices, but never in the living quarters. I located my cell and my name was on the door. It was handwritten and appeared almost permanent. I like that name for a room—*cell*—but I couldn't help but think about how I'd spent a lifetime trying to keep my clients out of them and especially ones with their name written permanently on the door. I got a lump in my throat before I even opened the door to my room. It was small inside and appointed simply, with a twin bed on the right, nestled snug against the wall. On the left side sat a compact desk and wooden chair, plus a chest for my clothing. A small crucifix hung alone on the back wall. On the bed was a blanket dating back to World War II, made of real wool with a U.S. Navy insignia. From my large picture window I could see the rolling meadow leading to the cemetery where I hope to one day be buried. I unpacked my bag and began unwinding. I was happy and at peace in the moment to be there in that room, my very own cell. I was also nervous. I was afraid I wouldn't be where I was supposed to be, when I was supposed to be there, or that I would say the wrong thing.

At 11:45 the bells rang for Sext, or midday prayers, and as I apprehensively made my way to the chapel I realized I didn't know where to go or sit. I had been going to this place for so long but not as a family brother. I hurried to find Brother Francis and he told me to follow him into the chapel. He pointed to a place in the choir stalls next to him—my place. I felt like Steve Martin's character in *The Jerk* when the new phone book arrived and he saw his name in print: "I'm somebody now!"

My first big mistake came after Compline when I saw Father Cyprian in the kitchen. I greeted him and told him how thrilled I was to be there. He smiled and very gently informed me that we observed the Great Silence after Compline until Vigils the next morning—that meant we didn't talk to each other. This rookie fumble could have been avoided if I'd read the Rule of Benedict more carefully. But of course Father Cyprian was gracious and kind about it; he could tell I was embarrassed.

I ate in the refectory and sat at my assigned seat for the main meals at noon. There was no talking, only listening to Brother Francis read a story or essay out loud from one of the great spiritual writers. Then everyone, including the abbot, pitched in to clean up after the meal.

Brother Francis posted work assignments on the central bulletin board for all of the monks each day. On this day I would be given the task of hand digging around a broken septic pipe about a mile from the monastery at the little hermitage used for monks on retreat. I was warned to watch out for the copperhead snakes under the house. It was rainy that day and the work was strenuous and fulfilling beyond measure. Father Paul's goal for me was to find the rhythm of the abbey and the Divine Hours. Rhythm is very important to this life.

The heart of the Benedictine Rule is summed up by *ora et labora*—prayer and work. They wanted me to experience this as a brother, not as a guest. I was expected to attend the prayer services of the Divine Hours, also called the Divine Office or Daily Office. These seven communal services are divided throughout the day to be balanced by work and individual prayer and study. There is a rhythm to the day, balancing work and prayer, that has been undisturbed for monasteries following the Rule for over fifteen centuries. The application of rhythm from monastic life to my life has required work, but the abbey is my guide. Obviously, I live in the world and not behind a cloister, but I know what the flow of the monastic day feels like and I aim for the essence of that flow in my Rule.

On my last day that fateful week, I met with Father Paul to further discuss my family brother candidacy. Father Paul, a former Yale and Princeton professor and accomplished author, outlined the path ahead for me. I related that one of my goals of the discipline was greater manifestation of the "fruits of the Spirit" in my own life as outlined in scripture: love, joy, peace, patience, kindness. And further, I wanted to see the face of Christ in all of the people I met. I was slightly taken aback when Father Paul explained that living in community as a family brother and making a vow was not a pop psychology workshop with the intention of becoming a "better person." I listened as we sat across the round table from one another, but his comment caught me off guard. He was trying to convey that while those "fruits" in my life were laudable, the monastic life that I was asking to share in was not in and of itself for this purpose. Father Paul filled the dead air by explaining that this was not an "ethic." He said that I would be unable to find these fruits or the face of Christ in others unless, as he put it, "you see the face of God in Jesus Christ."

Aha. The recipe of monastic life was pointing me beyond the "flavor" of kindness (or gentleness, etc.) and toward the larger dish, the greater purpose—in my case, the Divine. And the Divine in me would reflect those things I hoped for. I had to trust this.

The purpose of my Rule was a life practice of loving God. Period. Father Paul taught me the paradox: if my objective of the Rule was to become a "better person," I would fail, but if my objective was to love God, then the qualities I wanted to develop as a person would naturally follow. Father Paul, knowing my history, was aware that he could gracefully push me to this end. The first bell rang, signaling midday prayers in five minutes. As we rose to walk to the church I felt refreshed and hopeful.

The Promise

My next step was to make a formal promise in front of the community after Vespers service one evening. "Can I do that this trip?" I inquired in the hallway just outside the door to the church. That would not be possible. Father Paul said there would need to be preparations, discussion with the abbot, and they would need to make my smock (sort of the monk's version of a hoodie). I was excited and ready to plan my next trip for a one-day visit and a promise. Not. So. Fast. I was reminded of a story I heard from Buddhist teacher Tara Brach. There was a young novice monk who, upon entering the monastery, asked the abbot how long it would take for him to encounter the Divine in a meaningful way. The abbot replied that it could take as long as ten years. "Ten years?" replied the monk, dejected. "What if I work really hard?" he asked. The abbot smiled and said, "For you, my son, it will be twenty." That's me. In case you're wondering, I started living my Rule even before it was finally approved. I figured if it was going to take me twenty years, I better get started.

After my visit I received a message from Father Paul that he had reviewed my Rule and found it "solid." The next day I traveled to the Philippines, just one day after a devastating typhoon hit Tacloban. Fortunately, our cocoa farmer partners were safe, unlike so many others. I met with the farmers about our next shipment of cocoa beans. When I returned to the States, I had a detailed discussion with Father Paul. I had assumed we were good to go with my proposed Rule of Life, but in February 2014 he told me that he and Brother Francis had discussed it and I needed to redraft it:

> *Thank you for sending me a copy of your Rule. I have discussed it with Br. Francis, and this is our response.*
>
> *Now, this is what you need yet to do: Make more concrete how you will live this lifestyle on a daily, weekly, maybe monthly and yearly*

*basis. Our concern is that you are a doing, doing, doing person, always
on the run, and the danger is to fit spiritual things in whenever, on the
way to something else, or in your car, etc. As you know, at the
monastery we live a schedule that gives a clear rhythm of being and
doing, not doing with inserted being. Therefore a good discipline for
you is to translate from your preamble a concrete schedule to which you
can be held accountable.*

*Without being unduly regimented or non-flexible, indicate when
you will rise, do what upon rising, spiritual activities (how long)
before leaving for work; any spiritual activities through the day (and
when); what will you do to close the day. Also how much reading per
week, frequency of church attendance, any need for disciplined
promises regarding diet, exercise, etc. I hope this gives you an idea of
what we have in mind. You don't have to make lots of promises, but
especially those that are especially needing to be done to counter some of
your weaker tendencies. I want to be able to picture a bit more just how
you really wish to live your life.*

If this is not clear, email me and Br. Francis, or call me.

You are doing well, and only need this one-step-more.

Prayers for you,

Fr. Paul

Really? I thought. *Do they not know who I am? I have been writing briefs
for courts all over the country for twenty years! First it was "solid" and now it's
not. It's not fair of them to go back and change their minds.* I never voiced these
things, thankfully, but the note stung. *I have spent decades in a profession
where people listen to me, sometimes even respect me,* I thought. *I have been a
dedicated guest of the abbey! Why can't they just get this part over with already?*
Crestfallen, I rolled my desk chair back from my monitor, took a
deep breath, and closed my eyes for a second. I stood up, grabbed my

phone and earbuds, and walked outside to my car, since the chocolate molding line was clanging away, like a thousand tiny church bells mocking my crappy Rule of Life.

As I dialed Father Paul I made sure to deeply breathe in a prayer for God's assistance so my frustration and sadness would remain hidden in my voice. I asked for more clarification. He said, "Shawn, we would like for you to find a state of being inserted by doing and not a state of doing inserted by being, and your Rule as written right now does not reflect that."

I remembered my discussion with Father Paul at the abbey. It had changed my view of everything. This statement was the essence of my practice. I started over from scratch. And I am so happy that Father Paul held my feet to the fire in his gentle and loving manner. They not only wanted to see evidence of balance in my Rule, they hoped my "doing" would be displaced by my "being." That by practicing "being," "doing" would follow. Rhythm, flow, and balance of *ora et labora* were all incorporated into this intention of being inserted by doing.

I sent them both another draft of my Rule of Life in February 2014, incorporating their detailed suggestions. On March first, Father Paul approved my Rule.

A few days later I traveled to the abbey to make my formal promise. At the end of Vespers service, in the presence of the community, I vowed to follow my Rule as best I could. I was nervous. I don't get nervous. Caron accompanied me to the altar and, hands shaking, I signed my Rule. The abbot also signed the document, then he presented me with my handmade smock, and I officially became a family brother.

I'll discuss my Rule—and how to craft your own—a bit later. First, I want to talk about retreats, solitude, and rhythm because they form a basic foundation for my spiritual practice and both my personal and business vocations.

Retreats: The Best-Kept Secret of Entrepreneurs (or Maybe Just Me)

You know the "corporate retreats" where everyone meets up in Cabo (or in my case, Branson) for a long weekend? There are meals and motivational speakers and team-building exercises. I'm sure those are fine, but the retreats I'm suggesting are for you. Just you. Alone.

When I'm feeling stuck, overwhelmed, or unsure of my next steps, a retreat to Assumption Abbey is just the thing I need. I've found it to be one of the most helpful things I can do for myself as a leader of a company. The monks call retreats "time apart from the busy world." It doesn't have to be a religious pursuit: you can still absolutely get a renewed sense of focus, clarity, and determination from going on retreat.

You may have guessed this by now, but I'm a type A guy. About as type A as they come. The abbey and my retreats there have helped round my type A corners, although this is still very much a work in progress. Going there is like taking steel wool to my rough spots. It's not always comfortable, sometimes it's even painful, but I always leave feeling more softened than I did before. Have I mentioned retreats and agendas are fairly incompatible? This is an important point that has probably been clear to most people seeking respite through retreats, but it took me a while to figure it out.

The best example to illustrate this point involves a difficult time when I was in a mini health crisis. Panicked, I endured MRIs, EMGs, and other tests, as well as follow-up visits with the neurologist and other doctors over a period of years. I was having trouble sleeping and felt fatigued most of the time. Nobody knew what was wrong. While I was struggling with this, I was constantly facing one of my biggest fears: that I would become sick and die while Lawren was still living at home. That she would inherit the same trauma that I had in losing my father as a teenager. That life would replay itself with her as the victim. Of course I recognized that this was unlikely, but that didn't dampen my overwhelming fear.

I visited the abbey during this time and the week before I arrived I had a conversation with God. I told Him I was going to be talking to Him about all of this when I was there. That I wanted some answers, some relief, and some rest. And that was not how my retreat went at all. I didn't even get much rest. God had other plans for my soul; namely, that Father Cyprian would explain the Paschal Mystery to me during one of our walks. This is the concept of Passover from slavery to the promised land; from dark to light; from death to life, death, and resurrection; it is regarded as a true mystery to be celebrated and even embraced. A mystery revealed by the graces of God, that I'm sure I'll be perplexed and fascinated by for the rest of my life. Needless to say, I've learned to adjust my expectations about retreats and over the years I've inherited some helpful tips.

If I were struggling with an important business decision, I don't think I would use a retreat to "figure it out." Having said that, many of the intricacies of our business vocation have resulted from my time at the abbey. That sounds like a contradiction, but it isn't. I did not go to the abbey, unpack my bag, sit in the chapel, and say, "God, do you think I should take on investors or sell the company?" Instead, I would go to the abbey, unpack, sit in the church, and say, "Here I am." I would walk, rest, pray, work (manual labor of some kind), read, pray—all in God's presence. Usually (but no promises) some ideas about decisions facing my company would rise up to the surface in the days following. How are retreats a good prescription for the entrepreneur? First, rest is good. Second, rest with intention is even better. It's powerful because intention magnifies the rest. And my intention shouldn't be to receive answers, but to have my heart and mind be open enough to receive them. Third, rest, intention, and time apart build a foundation for clarity.

My relationship with the abbey, finding my faith again—this all began with a retreat. So, what makes for a good retreat?

One of the best pieces of advice came to me from my friend Tobias, who is a self-described Buddhist Catholic. Toby suggested that a week before a retreat was scheduled to begin I take one part of my daily schedule, like lunch, and make a slight change. He said I should try soup or some other food I might not normally eat, with the intention that this change would be a physical manifestation of my intention to be on retreat the following week and rest in God's presence. Why do I agree, and pass this advice along to you? Because this act tends to give us a slight pause in our very busy daily lives and give a portion of gratitude and mindfulness to what's coming up. It is a micro retreat that foreshadows and prepares you for what will be. This minor alteration to your routine could be anything as long as it's aligned with your intention. It could be something as simple as reading a few lines of poetry before bed a week before the retreat.

Most of my biggest personal and business decisions have been intertwined with a retreat: working with palliative care patients, changing careers, staying small, using reverse scale, taking students to Tanzania, starting school lunch programs, and setting the overall way of being for our business. The most important aspect of my business that retreats have solidified over the years? The way in which we harmonize our need for profitability with our desire to serve.

Much of what I am saying in this book is countercultural to traditional business—from defining "enough," to reverse scale, to our view of profit and goodness. In order to swim against the tide we need help and in some cases we need a lifeline. The abbey, the Rule, and retreats have been that for me. As an entrepreneur it would be impossible for me to find my way on the winding trail that leads to the present moment but for the work and practice described here.

Considerations for Your Retreat

There are monasteries all over the world with guest housing for those seeking a retreat. There are over forty Benedictine and thirteen Trappist monasteries with guest ministries in America alone. A quick search will reveal many Buddhist monasteries and retreat centers in the United States. The possibilities are endless and often inexpensive, with some requesting only a donation and others a nominal fee. My abbey will even try to make arrangements to pick you up at the airport, which is an hour and a half away. Guests are very important in all monasteries because in most contemplative traditions hospitality is a critical facet of spirituality. The Benedictine Rule, for example, devotes an entire chapter to the topic, stating, "Any guest who happens to arrive at the monastery should be received just as we would receive Christ himself." Wherever you are there is probably some kind of retreat center hidden near you. You might be wondering if a retreat necessitates staying at a religious guesthouse. Of course not. You could stay home and have a retreat. You could check in at your local Four Seasons for a memorable retreat, I am sure—or a Hampton Inn or something, which is more my speed. Likewise you may ask if it's okay to go to a religious place for a retreat, even if you're not religious. The answer in general is yes, though you should of course do plenty of research on any given place, to make sure it's a good fit for you, and that you won't find their religious approach alienating. Whatever your beliefs, there are some considerations:

1. What is your true intention for the retreat? Is it rest and relaxation only? Do you desire "rest in God's presence," otherwise known as contemplative prayer? If God is not the focus of your retreat, what is? Your intention will guide your decision about location.

2. Do you have the discipline to tune out the distractions of a hotel? Wi-Fi and TV and the things to do in the neighborhood are just a few of the potential distractions that can take my mind away from a retreat.

3. Remember that monastic guesthouses are not listed on the Small Luxury Hotels of the World registry. The consideration is whether or not you're going to be satisfied with a skimpy mattress on a twin bed, simple food, a tiny room, sometimes a shared restroom, no TV, no Wi-Fi, and a built-in wake-up call in the form of bells at 3:15 a.m.

4. Finally, there is a benefit to retreat centers at religious sites even if you're not interested in something religious or spiritual, and it is that you are in a place where other people have gone before (in some cases for decades or centuries) with similar intentions. You'll be in a place where fellow retreatants are doing the same things you are. This shared seeking and resting is holy and contributes to the overall experience of a retreat.

Upon arrival at the abbey it takes me at least twenty-four hours to unwind and overcome technology withdrawal. I like to stay on a retreat for at least four full days. Within forty-eight hours I can finally begin to feel the rhythm. But these are only guidelines, not expectations; they can vary and you'll need to see what's true for you.

These days I try not to grade myself on the success of a retreat. In a weird way, I find many snippets of peace even in the unrest and I think it's because I stay true to the practice. Anyone can go on a retreat when life is wonderful and find rest. That's easy. The harder, but more fulfilling, thing is finding rest on retreat when life or business sucks. Those are the lessons you can really take with you.

The other thing about retreats is that the results I want to feel immediately don't always come. I have found, though, that the effects of my time at the abbey inevitably appear in my life and business later. In fact, if there is a goal of the retreat—and I am not really in favor of having "goals" for retreats—it is that I rest in God's presence and later the fruit of that rest will manifest itself in the details of my relationships and my business.

It's kind of like planting a garden. When you plant seed, it doesn't immediately produce food. We till, plant, tend, water, and weed and then one day we see that there is something from our work: food we can eat. At least for me most retreats are like this. We hope that our tending to practice resting in God's presence in prayer, meditation, working, and reading will bring us closer to Him and in turn closer to everyone and everything else in future days.

I try to bring the abbey with me when I leave it. My friend Toby says that he keeps the abbey in his heart and that way it's always there. He does this by practicing resting in God's presence every day and not just during times of retreat. I have tried to do this, too, over the years. As with everything else, some years I'm better at it than others. Ultimately, what I hope for is that my behavior in the world is congruent with my practice and belief. If not, then what's the point? We all want our actions to bear out our beliefs. The abbey is a holy place of humble prayer that resembles a living, breathing entity. Within its walls it holds decades of worship offered to God and petitions of need and thanksgiving breathed into the stained glass, rooms, and trees. There's an energy, a sense of camaraderie, with all those who've retreated before you and will retreat after you, with the monks, that provides a unifying calm.

What about group retreats? If your leadership team is open to a weekend retreat with an agenda I think that is a great idea. Most, if not all, of the exercises in this book could be accomplished at a group retreat. What about the incompatibility of agendas and retreats?

This is different because it's not as much about communicating with the Divine, or other kinds of contemplation, as it is about communicating with each other.

The Business of Solitude

My business benefits from my times of solitude, but that's not my reason for seeking it. As a collaborative entrepreneur I love input from all sides and always have. As a businessperson, solitude is not my default setting and it does not come naturally. The practice of solitude is a training ground for listening to the voice in your head. That's the voice of fear, panic, anxiety, and depression. It's also the voice of courage, peace, creativity, and joy. I need to distinguish all of those voices as an entrepreneur in order to make good decisions.

Unplugging is critical to achieving solitude. I'm not suggesting you unplug all the time, but selecting intentional moments, days, or weeks to take a break from technology is crucial. It allows the opportunity to rest in God's presence and become our true selves. And it inevitably gives clarity to our business vocation. Of course, it's also extremely challenging because we're so dependent on technology.

Unplugging is a proposition with many possibilities. Does that mean abstaining from e-mail for a set period of time? Or not engaging in social media? Does it mean no computers at all? No technology? Retreats are the most opportune time to unplug. For me it's easy because there's no Wi-Fi (so no social media, no e-mail, and no browsing), no cell signal (so no texting or calling), but I use my camera and listen to music. Ultimately, it's impossible to *really* retreat if you don't unplug in some way because you miss out on solitude. Unplugging isn't easy if you've got access, but with commitment and a plan it can happen.

Thomas Merton makes a great point in one of my favorite books, *The Sign of Jonas*: "Silence and solitude are the supreme luxuries of life!" Merton posits that you don't actually have to go on a retreat to find this luxury. "Solitude is not found so much by looking outside the boundaries of your dwelling, as by staying within. Solitude is not something you must hope for in the future. Rather, it is a deepening of the present, and unless you look for it in the present you will never find it." In other words, I can have every intention of finding it in next month's retreat, but never discover it because I'm not searching for it in the here and now.

If solitude is a state of mind then it can be cultivated and practiced anywhere, even at work once you've become adept at it. My greatest impediment to solitude is the distraction of work. I can always take up one more thing of work to occupy the uncomfortable solitude that is creeping. And unfortunately technology makes that distraction as simple as breathing. This is why being on a retreat with no access to technology works so well for me.

Solitude is also frightening, which makes us less inclined to pursue it. Merton concludes, "Solitude means being lonely not in a way that pleases you but in a way that frightens and empties you to the extent that it means being exiled even from yourself."

Okay, great! Sound like fun yet? So far solitude is a luxury, it's lonely and frightening, and you're not going to achieve it by hoping for it tomorrow. But there's no need to sugarcoat the idea of solitude. If you've never experienced it, you're in for some pain and suffering. Then why this path? What's the benefit? The value is that solitude is the space where we can best unearth our true selves. The retreat setting, in my case the abbey, primes me for solitude in a way that my undisciplined life cannot. Also, for me, solitude feels a little less lonely when there are other people around, doing the same thing. The abbey in the wilderness prepares me in body, mind, and spirit to find solitude.

For me, retreats have not necessarily been about receiving answers, even though I have often attempted to make them about that. Now I have come to believe that they are about resting in God's presence, via contemplative prayer (for some, another way of defining solitude). The idea is to empty yourself so that God can fill that space. Sometimes, when rest is not possible, then it's about *practicing* resting. "Be still and know that I am God" is one of my favorite psalms and a very challenging proposition at times. The first part—be still—is not an easy instruction for most to follow. Being alone with our thoughts can be frightening and when we're still we sometimes realize there are big things stirring in our heads, our hearts, our souls. These "big things" are important but we avoid hearing them because they can be disconcerting or frightening. We avoid stillness at all costs, even to the point of conditioning ourselves to prevent it from being part of daily life.

Why should I be still so all those thoughts and fears can chase each other around in my head, bringing on more suffering? The reason for me is that there's a second half to the psalm: know that I am God. While being alone in my thoughts can be uncomfortable at times I find, through practice, that there is no fear in the present moment if I can be still and know that God is God, not me. On retreat what this means is that during a dark time of my life I might not sleep well, so I wake up and practice. By practice I mean attending most, if not all, of the prayer services that begin at 3:30 a.m. with Vigils. Then I might take a hike, or sit and watch the river, and then it starts: racing thoughts in my head and I can't calm myself enough to even pray. I've learned not to let the racing thoughts overwhelm me, to allow myself to sit with them and continue my practice. At the end of the retreat sometimes I don't feel rested at all. At first I used to think as I was packing up my car to go home: *Really? I spend all of this time and You can't give me some rest and answers?*

"Contemplative prayer" is the term for a variety of methods, in a variety of monastic faith traditions, which can result in divine union with God. Buddhism, Judaism, Islam, Hinduism, and I'm sure others have monastic prayer practices. Several of these traditions use chanting, for instance. One way I think of contemplative practice is like this: In *Enter the Dragon*, Bruce Lee tells his student, "It is like a finger pointing away to the moon. Don't concentrate on the finger or you will miss all that heavenly glory." I'm certain that all the religious monastic prayer practices of the world would agree with Bruce.

There are comparable nonreligious contemplative practices. Meditation is one. Another is something called yoga nidra, or what experts call "yogic sleep." I do this practice sometimes in order to enhance my prayer life, but I am by no means an expert; this is purely my personal experience of it. As my novice mind understands it, the purpose of yoga nidra is not divine union with anyone. It is a state of consciousness in deep sleep. I have found it to be deeply relaxing. The practitioner lies in corpse pose and, using meditation techniques far beyond the scope of this book, remains awake but in a state of stillness that is beyond the conscious mind. However, yoga nidra is not the same thing as meditation. If you are interested in this practice I strongly encourage you to research "advanced" or "authentic" yoga nidra and not use the app—yes, there's an app! I tried it and it didn't seem like much more than a relaxing meditation. Yoga nidra is one method of emptying oneself, but there are certainly others you could seek out, from other traditions.

Despite the occasional pain of solitude, the scarcity of tidy answers, and the time it takes to cultivate, it remains a potent practice in life and in business. The ceaseless tidal wave of all this technology, connectivity, and "always on" lifestyle implores us to push back and purposefully find solitude so that we may operate our business (both professionally and personally) with mindfulness and intention.

Rhythm—a New Kind of Schedule

Roman Catholic monks around the world pray the Divine Office, or the Liturgy of the Hours—which is to say, at regular intervals all day long, every day. While the actual times can vary slightly depending on the abbey, it looks like this at Assumption Abbey: Vigils at 3:30 a.m.; Lauds and Mass at 6:30 a.m.; Terce at 9:00 a.m.; Sext at 11:45 a.m.; None at 2 p.m.; Vespers at 5:45 p.m.; Compline at 7:45 p.m. These prayer services occur at approximately three-hour intervals and each has a different focus.

I have a practice that helps maintain this rhythm when I'm not at the abbey. I set a series of gentle bells that ring on my phone at the times of the Daily Office (minus the 3:30 a.m. Vigils bells because, well, I have enough trouble sleeping as it is). These are set to ding five times per day and I know exactly what the monks are doing when I hear the bells. It stops me and sometimes even jolts me, which is exactly what I need. Each time I hear the bells, I stop whatever activity I'm in the middle of and say a tiny prayer suggested to me by Father Paul: "With you, O Christ, I live in hope." I don't say it out loud; I don't get on my knees or go anywhere. I just pause briefly, close my eyes, and say it silently to myself, then resume what I was doing but hopefully with more peace.

It's meant to be a reminder of my intentions during my day. You could do the same thing for a short time with any prayer or intention that suits you. My business day can be chaotic and this very simple reminder while I'm at work can gently but firmly reel me back to the place I need to be. Any entrepreneur could benefit from a tool like this that whispers, "Hey, you, that thing you just said, the tack you're on: not so much."

The daily life of the monk's work and prayer centers on the rhythm of this practice of the Divine Hours every single day. This daily schedule is significant. On the surface, it literally explains the monks' activities, day in and day out. At its heart, though, this schedule represents so much more: the importance of daily work rhythm, finding contentedness (and prayer) in routine, simplicity, and the impact of creating a thoughtful day, with intention, which allows for peace and tranquillity. Moreover, the practice of contemplation and resting in God's presence does lend itself to peace in the moment of worship and prayer, but the deeper result is found in everyday life.

Rhythm is not as much about "work-life balance" for me as it is about the parts of my life that coexist with my work, my business. Rhythm is not an end, but a means by which I can construct my day, week, year. My friend Ari says that he does not know what "work-life balance" means—that it's all life. I know what he means because in my business taking local students to Tanzania is part of my life and it is inseparable from my work. But there is rhythm in that project throughout the year that follows a schedule—and it's intertwined with selling chocolate.

Routines Create Rhythm

Like the monks, I try to follow a daily routine as it relates to my Rule. I wake up around 6:30 each day. I get ready for work (which does not take too long since I wear the same thing every day), go to our little home office, which is off of our bedroom, light a candle, and start a tiny amount of incense (the same that is used at the abbey). I do some yoga stretches to loosen up and to wake up. I follow the Catholic lectionary and begin my prayers. I use the Ignatian Spiritual Exercises, developed by St. Ignatius of Loyola. They are meant to immerse you in the scripture reading of the day. For example, the passage of scripture is read and then you're asked to imagine yourself in the scene. There is an aspect of meditation and contemplation to this prayer exercise. On some mornings I will also follow this with either Centering Prayer, which is a simple "resting in God's presence," for about 15 minutes, or the restorative yoga pose called waterfall. On weekend mornings sometimes I use Sound-Cloud and follow along with the Daily Office of morning prayer. During the day my phone will ring a Tibetan bell for the hours of the Daily Office and as I've mentioned, I pause and bring my mind to the mantra "With you, O Christ, I live in hope." Is it a little weird when the bell dings and I am watching *Keeping Up with the Kardashians* with my wife (we love reality television)? Yes, but that's the idea—to be reminded to be centered no matter what I am doing.

In the evening before bed I end the day with the Examen, which is a guided examination of the day and my interaction with it, both good and bad. Where did I see God? Where did I represent Him well and where did I not? Then I follow a guided prayer for the next day. Many evenings I do Compline, which is the last prayer service of the day. The monks use it as a chance to pray for a restful night and a peaceful death. Obviously the peaceful death part resonates with me. The service I follow is the one recorded and uploaded to SoundCloud that evening by my priest, Father David, of St. John's Episcopal Church.

I keep a work routine as well. When I am in town, upon arrival at the factory, I first visit with our production team and make an effort to speak to each person. I taste the chocolate we are molding for the day and I visually inspect the bars. If we are roasting, I taste the beans. All of this occurs pretty quickly depending on issues that come up. Then I head to our offices. I quickly dispense with the morning's e-mail in a matter of minutes. I make a second cup of coffee in my cubicle and read the news. I almost always bring my lunch and eat alone in my car and listen to uplifting podcasts. Most of my meetings are scheduled in the afternoon. The most important meetings of the week are on Tuesdays, and have been for as long as I can remember, because I love Tuesdays (because of Morrie!). I often meet with friends, business acquaintances, and students around 4:00 p.m. for tea at a nearby coffee shop. I'm always home by 6:00 p.m.

That's pretty ordinary, but the rhythm I've created is central to my ability to do so many things (and still watch *Friday Night Lights* or *Gilmore Girls* when I'm home from work). I also wear a "uniform" every day: chambray work shirt and jeans. My routine is predictable and a comfort; it eliminates unnecessary distractions because I have to make fewer choices. My routine allows me to be more productive. Most entrepreneurs are familiar with decision fatigue and a routine significantly reduces that pesky problem. Do I miss out on opportunities sometimes? Perhaps, but I am willing to miss some things that come my way in order to have rest and experience joy.

Writing Your Own Rule of Life

My own Rule of Life incorporates a version of this rhythm of balance. As a reminder, my complete Rule is listed at the back of this book in appendix C—not because it's a masterpiece, but only to offer a template for seekers around the world to use in writing their own. I include it because in my research I couldn't find much on crafting your own Rule, especially as it related to the original Rule of Benedict.

The Rule comprises four parts: prayer, study, recreation or enjoyment, and work. At the end of the Rule, I outline my daily, weekly, monthly, and annual schedule. That is where the rubber meets the road. It's easy to write platitudes about how I intend to live my life, but not so easy to daily transform my life into a "state of being inserted by doing." On a monthly basis I meet with someone, usually a friend who understands my Rule, and this person asks me questions about how I am doing with keeping to my Rule. This is not a cross-examination but a conversation; part confession and part affirmation.

My Rule is very personal and detailed, but not meant to be lawyerly and rigid. I am open about relationships and work. There were and are some very specific areas of my life that needed and need help. For instance, sometimes I can be a jerk to the people I care most about. (There, I said it.) But I don't want to be that kind of a person and all of the excuses in the world are just that. As stated in my Rule, "I have faith that grace will find the still point within me where God resides and that everything else in the world—no matter the pace and apparent chaos—will revolve around it." Nice, but it doesn't always work that way.

So then what do you do? I confessed to Father Paul recently that I've been committed in my practice but lately the fruits of kindness and gentleness were lost in the depths of my lopsided work schedule. He told me that my awareness of the issue was great, that I should be gentle on myself and keep with it. He confirmed what I already know—that this will be a lifelong struggle for me. More specifically he gave me direction about what to do during my stay at the abbey: "Don't give yourself reading assignments; relax, go into the church when you arrive, center yourself, focus on an object in your hand (a cross or rosary), and just be and do this over and over again." Just be. Simple but great advice. In case you hadn't noticed, I have not arrived at some euphoric place as passing through a heretofore locked gate. Instead, this is a path toward radical balance for me and sometimes it's foggy and I lose my way. Fortunately, I have people around me to help me back onto the path—people in my family, trusted friends, a spiritual director, and a monastic community. All of this is for a purpose and it's not so I can win the piety button for the year.

If you want to write and live by a Rule, these are the basics:

1. An introduction that states why you want a Rule to begin with. What is the purpose? Be specific. This is not a New Year's resolution list.

2. What is the basis of your Rule? Is it your faith or is it anchored in something else? As mentioned, the basis of my Rule is loving God. But yours does not have to be about spiritual beliefs. It should, though, be about something beyond you.

3. Choose the main areas of your life that you want to balance and why. I like to give the details of what that will actually look like.

4. What is your daily, monthly, and annual schedule to live out the Rule? What routines will you create? And how will you maintain rhythm?

5. Pick some people you can meet with regularly to hold you to the Rule. These people are not your judges but encouragers who are interested in your life and are willing to ask you difficult questions.

6. Update—or at least review—your Rule annually. I updated my Rule after six months and then after one year. The reason for updating is that as life changes I find that tools that once helped no longer serve me, so I use other tools to point me toward a greater interior life. I will update my Rule every year and some years make major changes and sometimes minor tweaks. Additionally, those friends who hold me accountable might change.

7. The main idea or center point of your Rule will not change. As you can see by now, I had trouble with this part even though I was pretty darn sure I knew what mine was. The monastic community I am part of helped immensely here because the structure and one-thousand-year history guided me along a well-worn path. Father Cyprian, Father Paul, and Brother Francis know me and I trust that they love me. In the long term it helps if your Rule is part of something bigger than yourself.

Rule of Life in Practice

One day, Father Cyprian and I were walking and talking, and the topic of my upcoming trip to Tanzania came up. He's very familiar with my business and specifically with our sustainable lunch program. He knows of my passion for helping to feed the malnourished children of this region in Tanzania. The conversation went on for a mile or more and he asked me, "What would you think about *waiting* to start another feeding program at another school until this one is totally sustainable and run by the school?"

He was, in his gentle way, asking me to wait to feed hungry children. How could he do that? Here's how: he knows that in order for me to live a life of radical balance in adherence to my Rule I must, despite what my heart and brain are telling me, wait to take on everything I want to accomplish. This waiting stuff is new to me. What possible benefit could there be in waiting? Well, the main one is preservation of myself physically and emotionally. Even humanitarian work—especially humanitarian work, because I fool myself into thinking that doing good things to help others is an exception—necessitates balance and patience.

These days I am constantly on guard and aware of my tendency toward activist philanthropy, knowing that I could easily fall back into the "doing" trap and ignore the restoration of my own soul. Good works are beautiful in the eyes of God but not if I am so exhausted that my little lamp's flame is extinguished.

Being inserted by doing. Meaning that I need to simply be. It's not relaxation, but a state of existence wherein I am calm, I am at peace, I breathe, I am intentional, mindful. It's very Buddhist. But also Christian—one of my favorite psalms is 46:10: "Be still and know that I am God." Then, in that state of being, I go about my day. I do things, I converse, I respond, I act, but all of the activity is essentially orbiting around a core of simply being. Am I that way? No! But it's my aspiration.

So I waited and didn't start a new program at a new school. And I won't until the first one thousand children are eating sustainably without our help. It was always our goal with this program for the community to no longer need us, Askinosie Chocolate, once we've guided them for a few years. This, to us, is true sustainability. But it's tough to wait. This is difficult for me and I think patience might not have been possible but for my Rule. The good news? That community is beginning to work together, even better than before, to take even more ownership of the program.

On another occasion of walking with Father Cyprian in the wilderness, I told him of an idea I have to start a sister business with our chocolate factory. I outlined the whole thing for him. He nodded as he listened for a couple of miles as I explained that it might take some of my time away from the chocolate factory to get this up and going. Remember, this is an eighty-six-year-old monk who can walk faster than I can. I thought he'd bought into the idea. We talked about several topics on our hike, most of them spiritual and about family. The next morning after Vigils at 4:30 a.m. he handed me a short, one-page note. In our sixteen years of friendship I can't recall any other time he handed me a note. Here is what it said:

> Shawn, I thought after yesterday's sharing (which may be beyond my limits)—your chocolate business is a success—but is still very young in years. You made a courageous step from one career to another with real risk, and are now on a steady keel. It is good to start looking ahead, but don't move too soon, otherwise it could be an impulse of instability.

An "impulse of instability"? I read that line over and over, even coming back to it hours later. At first I felt defensive, but that didn't last long. After contemplation I understood what he meant, because stability is central to monastic life in all faith traditions. It is one of the most important vows a monk or nun can make. The Trappist website puts it like this:

> By our vow of stability, we promise to commit ourselves for life to one community of brothers or sisters with whom we will work out our salvation in faith, hope, and love. Resisting all temptation to escape the truth about ourselves by restless movement from one place to the next, we gradually entrust ourselves to God's mercy experienced in the company of brothers or sisters who know us and accept us as we are.

Father Cyprian was telling me not to move restlessly on to the next new endeavor, but instead to sit, for a while, with things as they were, in order to be able to look at myself honestly.

Later that morning, after a few hours of meditation on the note, I talked to Father Cyprian and explained that I was originally taken aback by his suggestion of instability. He replied, "It was once said that a good pastor makes the comfortable uncomfortable and the uncomfortable comfortable." We both laughed. I thanked him profusely for his candor and willingness to be a real friend and spiritual director. Needless to say, I put the brakes on my plans and slowed them way down. This, again, was very difficult for me as an entrepreneur whose head is a veritable idea factory that keeps me awake at night. My Rule, my desire to live by it, and my relationship with Cyprian set me on a different course. To live a Rule we need people to help us, and while my family and close friends know my Rule well, it's beneficial to have someone outside of this circle who can help hold me accountable.

Finally, why do you think Father Cyprian, at some point during every conversation we've had for sixteen years, has asked me, "What does Caron think?" or "Have you discussed this with Caron?" It's because Cyprian knows my soul and, truth be told, has a better understanding of my need for balance than I do myself. He wants me to balance my vocation of justice and compassion for others with the same action at home—the part of my Rule that I tend to struggle with the most. It was Mother Teresa who said, "It is easy to love the people far away. It is not always easy to love those close to us."

One day, Father Cyprian will die. Of course, I have no idea when that will be; he's not sick or anything. But I figure since I have this fear of death, why not apply it to other people, too, right? When I look at my relationship with Father Cyprian—everything I've learned from him; the hours he has given to help me craft and follow my Rule, and love God, and do my work well; even my fear of losing him—in essence, it can all be reduced to this: I want to be like him. Yes, I know he's human and imperfect like all of us. But I pray that someday I can answer someone's simple question of "How are you doing?" in the same way he does: to look the person in the eye with a genuine smile and say, "I am flourishing!"

APPENDIX A

BREAKING DOWN THE SUPPLY CHAIN CYCLE: WHAT DO COCOA FARMERS ACTUALLY MAKE?

For us, profit sharing with farmers is part of the supply chain cycle. At the beginning of the cycle is the actual price paid for beans; this price is critical. Let's break down the price of cocoa beans in order to understand what farmers actually make. Many chocolate makers around the world make some variation of this statement: "We pay farmers above the Fair Trade price for our cocoa beans." Some take this price bragging to new heights. A New York City chocolate maker said in a 2012 video that they have paid as much as ten times the "market price" for beans and most of the time they pay three to five times above market price. First of all, market price refers to the world commodities price listed on the New York or London commodities exchange. Second, why would anyone make "price to farmer" claims? Well, because we all want to appear fair and actually *be* fair to farmers around the world. Fair prices are beneficial for the supply chain's overall sustainability and fairness to farmers is a moral imperative.

Here's the world cocoa farmer story in one paragraph: The World Cocoa Foundation estimates that 80 to 90 percent of the world's cocoa supply comes from 5 to 6 million smallholder cocoa farmers (about five to ten acres).[1] Most

---

1 http:// worldcocoafoundation.org/ wp-content/ uploads/ Cocoa-Market -Update-as-of-4-1-2014.pdf.

cocoa farmers live at or near poverty, defined by the United Nations as per capita earnings below $1.90 per day,[2] and some live below it in what is considered extreme poverty, below $1.25 per day.[3] You might say, "So do a lot of farmers. Why should I care about cocoa farmers in particular?" You should care because we enjoy chocolate and chocolate comes from cocoa beans. The U.S. chocolate market alone is on track to hit $25 billion by 2019.[4] However, the bad news for farmers is that there's been no—as in zero—change in the commodity price in the last thirty years when adjusted for inflation.[5] Arguably, the price has actually gone down when adjusted for inflation.[6] To make matters worse, yields have not improved much in the last thirty years. This means that the price paid to farmers is essentially unchanged since you and I had our first [fill-in-the-blank] chocolate bar when we were kids.

The price paid to farmers is called "farm gate" price: what they actually receive in hand at the gate of their farm. The average cocoa farmer receives between 53 percent and 60 percent of the commodity price at the farm

---

2 http://www.un.org/sustainabledevelopment/poverty/.

3 The World Cocoa Foundation states that the average cocoa farmer has between two and four hectares (five to ten acres), yielding between 300 and 400 kg per hectare in Africa, 400 kg per hectare in Asia, and 600 kg per hectare in the Americas (http://worldcocoa foundation.org/wp-content/uploads/Cocoa-Market-Update-as-of-4-1-2014.pdf). At the time of writing, the ICCO spot commodity price is hovering around $3,000 per metric ton, and farmers receive a farm gate price on average of about 70 percent of the world commodity price (in some cases much lower). If we say the average yield is 450 kg per hectare, the typical farmer family will receive $3,307 per year, or $9.06 per day; divided by 6 (assuming six people in the family), this equals $1.51 per person per day. Shockingly, according to the Cocoa Barometer 2015 report (p.1), over 2 million farmers in Ghana and Ivory Coast are earning about $0.84 and $0.50 per day respectively.

4 http://www.mintel.com/press-centre/food-and-drink/us-chocolate-market-on-track -to-hit-25-billion-in-2019-lags-behind-europe-in-product-innovation.

5 http://www.indexmundi.com/commodities/?commodity=cocoa-beans&months=360.

6 The commodity price of one metric ton of cocoa beans in 1985 was $2,342.19. In today's dollars that would be $5,187.56, according to the Bureau of Labor Statistics CPI Inflation Calculator. The price today for one metric ton is roughly $3,000. Therefore, the price has actually decreased!

gate.[7] However, most of the world's cocoa farmers, who live in West Africa, receive well below that. For example, in Ghana and Ivory Coast (about 70 percent of the world's total supply) the farmers in February 2015 received about 55 percent and 50 percent of the commodity price respectively.[8] Eight trading companies in the world control the world cocoa bean supply, and six chocolate companies comprise 40 percent of the total market share.[9] This market concentration is what I call "Big Cocoa." Meanwhile the demand for chocolate is rising rapidly. Big Cocoa predicts a 1 million metric ton shortfall of cocoa beans by 2020. The Big Cocoa answer to this predicament is more farmers, more trees, and more yield to supply rising demand. As a manufacturer I can tell you that just because you can make more of something, it does not always mean more net profit. Variable costs increase with higher yields so I don't buy, ipso facto, that more yield equals more disposable income for farmer families. Big Cocoa markets a consumer-facing "Cocoa Action" plan for "better" lives for farmers. NGOs are complicit in this plan for more farmers, more trees, and more yield. Bringing more cocoa bean supply into the marketplace might fend off fears of a shortage, but it will also drive bean prices down. Big Cocoa's boot remains on the necks of poor cocoa farmers, holding them down but letting up just enough for them to catch a breath. In short, they are kept in place—right where the big players want them. All of this cumulates in a very weak negotiating position for farmers around the world.

---

7 According to Ed Seguine, renowned cocoa expert and member of the World Cocoa Foundation Fine Flavor Committee, the "Cocoa Action Working Group on Farm Economics is using a farm gate price of 53–60 percent of world price." From e-mail to the author, November 2, 2015.

8 The February 2015 world market price for cocoa beans was $2,947 per metric ton (http://www.icco.org/statistics/cocoa-prices/monthly-averages.html) and the farmers of Ghana and Ivory Coast received $1,630 per ton and $1,487 per ton respectively at the farm gate (http://www.cocoabarometer.org/International_files/Cocoa%20Barometer%202015%20USA.pdf).

9 http://www.cocoabarometer.org/International_files/Cocoa%20Barometer%202015%20USA.pdf.

What is the solution? The answer is that the price of beans at the farm gate needs to be higher, much higher. This will not happen without a supply shortage. First—and this is radical, I know—I believe that some cocoa farmers need to stop farming cocoa and move toward other crops that will bring them more money. The effect will also create a shortage of beans and higher price. Secondly, we should do everything we can to encourage production, sale, and consumption of chocolate products in origin countries. Production at origin alone is not enough. Higher demand for cocoa-related consumption at the origin is key. This will also create bean shortages, which will increase bean prices, and benefit local origin economies.

Finally, Big Cocoa should profit share with cocoa farmers. Hershey recorded over $7 billion in sales for 2014.[10] Sharing 1 percent with their farmers worldwide would be $70 million to split with the roughly 7 percent of the world's cocoa farmers, or 420,000 farmers (Hershey controls roughly 7 percent of the global market[11])—that's $166 to each farmer. That might not sound like much, but for those who earn $1.90 per day, it's huge. That's a 24 percent increase in their annual income.

The bottom line is that the price of cocoa beans could rise significantly before it would erode profit margins on chocolate bars. Furthermore, the price of chocolate bars—and I mean all chocolate bars, from what you buy at the convenience store to my chocolate bars—should be higher, much, much higher. Chocolate is price inelastic, meaning that as the price goes up, demand does not go down.[12] And the claim that we in the premium chocolate category, who pay more for high-quality beans, will eventually affect the price paid to farmers around the world is a pipe dream and will never happen. The reason is that there will never be enough buyers of high-

---

10 http://www.statista.com/statistics/235932/total-global-chocolate-sales-of-the -hershey-company/.

11 http://www.bloomberg.com/bw/magazine/content/10_04/b4164036499160.htm (albeit 2010 information, but the general picture of pie split remains).

12 http://www.marketwatch.com/story/chocolate-lovers-get-ready-to-pay-up-2014-07-25.

quality beans; our effect is infinitesimal now and it won't ever move the needle. Yes, we should insist on quality and it should be rewarded, but *all* cocoa farmers need to be getting more money for their beans *regardless of quality.*

The answer is not letting Big Cocoa off the hook because they've built schools and clinics or trained farmers to increase yields or spent donor dollars on NGOs who carry out the well-meaning plans of Big Cocoa. The answer is a dramatically higher farm gate price. This declaration is easy to make but difficult to practice because what I am proposing could hurt my business. As I said, we can absorb the margin hit with a higher farm gate price. The problem for us will be whether or not we have the cash flow to handle the higher cost of the cocoa beans.

What We Pay Our Farmers

Farm gate price is important to us because it's an apples-to-apples comparison point that we use. Every single bean purchase we've made in our history has exceeded the average farm gate price by at least 18.8 percent. Not surprisingly, as noted in appendix B, our contract price paid (including profit share) has been on average 48 percent greater than the average farm gate price since we started buying cocoa beans! That is real money in the pockets of farmers. In over twenty-six shipments of bean crops we've received, we have shared nearly $80,000 in profits directly with farmers (more, by the time you're reading this). It's important to note that the world commodity price includes physical delivery of the beans to New York. The price we pay farmers does not include delivery to a U.S. port; that's another fee we have to pay the shipping company, freight forwarders, and customs brokers. And if we use the commodity price per ton as our benchmark for discussion, then nobody really knows what the farmer receives. If we use the Fair Trade premium on top of the commodity price, we still don't know what the farmer receives. One can claim to "pay" farmers ten times the market price but we don't know who gets what. It is very common that the farmer will sell to a buying agent who then sells to another agent who sells to an export company who then sells to one of the eight multinational buyers who dominate and control the cocoa bean commodity sector. We've posted every individual contract and every price since inception in appendix B.

This level of transparency in the cocoa supply chain is unprecedented, but that's not what motivated us to release the data below. We're sharing this information for two reasons: because we think our customers deserve it and because we want to hold ourselves accountable. Are we delivering the value we say we are? After ten years of being in business, we felt it was important to assess ourselves, analyze our history, and figure out how we can improve. We owe it to our customers, who trust us, and we owe it to ourselves. We're always striving to do better, be more transparent, make connections, and share more, with our customers, our farmer partners, and each other. One way we're working to improve is by monitoring farm gate pricing even more closely. We also want to continue to improve cocoa bean quality. We can't just share profits because we're obligated to, we must share also as an incentive to harvest and ferment the beans with excellence, care, and attention to detail.

We must continue to sidestep the trap of complacency. After all, we have strong relationships with our farmer partners and awards for the chocolate bars made with their beans. But that thinking is a slippery slope to lesser bean quality, and thus lower-quality chocolate. Together with our farmer partners we will continue to innovate, think creatively, and be bold.

ASKINOSIE BEAN PURCHASE HISTORY

Conclusions

1. The contract price we pay plus the profit share we pay is on average 48 percent greater than the average farm gate price.

2. Every cocoa bean purchase we've ever made has exceeded the average farm gate price by at least 18.8 percent.

3. In the past ten years we've paid farmers on average 39.13 percent above world market price and 29.92 percent above Fair Trade price.

4. The profit share at each origin is essentially 10 percent net profit or 1 percent gross revenue for that year's crop.

5. At the time of writing, we have profit shared nearly $80,000 with farmers on twenty-six crops of beans.

6. Since 2005, we have paid over $1,000,000 to farmers in total (cocoa bean purchases plus profit shares).

7. We've provided financing to farmers in 64 percent of all bean transactions over the last ten years by making advance payments with 0 percent interest charged to the farmers.

8. For more definitions, descriptions, and details on the information contained in this chart, please visit Askinosie.com (https://www.askinosie.com).

ASKINOSIE CHOCOLATE COCOA BEAN

ORIGIN	CONTRACT YEAR	BEAN COST PER METRIC TON	PROFIT SHARE PER METRIC TON [10]	TOTAL PAID DIRECT TO FARMERS PER METRIC TON	COMPARABLE FARM GATE PRICE [3, 6]
ECUADOR	2006	$2,300.00	$319.37	$2,619.37	$2,204.59 [5]
	2008	$3,200.00	$188.30	$3,388.30	$2,116.40 [5]
	2010	$3,542.86	$166.10	$3,708.96	$2,855.38 [5]
	2011	$3,500.00	$166.10	$3,666.10	$2,855.38 [5]
	2012	$2,960.00	$532.00	$3,492.00	$2,645.50 [5]
	2013	$3,100.00	$458.47	$3,558.47	$2,314.81 [5]
	2014	$4,065.41	$285.02	$4,350.43	$2,755.73 [5]
	2015	$4,222.22	$500.00	$4,722.22	$3,086.42 [5]
	2016	$4,290.00	$0.00 [1]	$4,290.00	$3,330.00 [5]
TOTAL					
AMAZONIA	2016	$3,958.94	$0.00 [1]	$3,958.94	$3,330.00
TOTAL					
PHILIPPINES	2008	$3,150.00	$530.57	$3,680.57	$1,775.92 [4]
	2010	$3,150.00	$388.74	$3,538.74	$2,183.29 [4]
	2011	$3,250.00	$382.83	$3,632.83	$2,208.18 [4]
	2012	$2,900.00	$390.67	$3,290.67	$2,676.30 [4]
	2013	$2,750.00	$0.00 [2]	$2,750.00	$2,714.88 [4]
	2015	$3,500.00	$245.57	$3,745.57	$2,918.11 [4]
	2016	$3,500.00	$395.59	$3,895.59	$2,754.05 [4]
	2017	$3,500.00	$0.00 [1]	$3,500.00	$3,120.00 [4]
TOTAL					
TANZANIA	2010	$2,614.76	$411.59	$3,026.35	$1,544.44 [7]
	2011	$3,491.97	$323.13	$3,815.10	$2,173.50 [7]
	2012	$3,000.00	$340.71	$3,340.71	$2,079.00 [7]
	2013	$2,750.00	$184.32	$2,934.32	$1,736.00 [7]
	2014	$3,007.69	$209.61	$3,217.30	$2,040.00 [7]
	2015	$3,222.22	$454.44	$3,676.66	$2,295.00 [7]
	2016	$3,000.00	$0.00 [1]	$3,000.00	$2,515.26 [7]
TOTAL					
MADAGASCAR [11]	2016	$11,060.00	$-	$11,060.00	
TOTAL					
INACTIVE ORIGINS					
HONDURAS	2010	$3,350.00	$407.00	$3,757.00	NA [12]
	2011	$3,350.00	$407.00	$3,757.00	
	2013	$2,348.03	$426.72	$2,774.75	
	2014	$3,400.00	$426.72	$3,826.72	
	2015	$3,140.00	$0.00 [1]	$3,140.00	
TOTAL					
MEXICO	2007	$1,750.00	$251.80	$2,001.80	Not available.
	2008	$2,789.94	$0.00 [2]	$2,789.94	
	2009	$3,590.05	$0.00 [2]	$3,590.05	
TOTAL					
VENEZUELA	2006	$3,196.71	$0.00 [2]	$3,196.71	NA [14]
TOTAL					
GRAND TOTAL					

TOTAL PAID TO FARMERS ABOVE COMPARABLE FARM GATE PRICE	TOTAL US DOLLARS FARMERS RECEIVED	SHAWN'S TRAVEL TO ORIGIN	TOTAL PAID TO FARMERS ABOVE WORLD MARKET PRICE [8]	TOTAL PAID TO FARMERS ABOVE FAIR TRADE PRICE [9]
18.81%	$15,716.20	October 2005, January 2006, May 2006	65.66%	51.31%
60.10%	$23,613.04	December 2007	50.44%	41.05%
29.89%	$14,144.00	April 2010	16.69%	11.43%
28.39%	$26,244.00	April 2010	25.23%	19.13%
32.00%	$24,444.00	April 2012	50.91%	38.91%
53.73%	$28,467.77	August 2013	29.16%	20.42%
57.87%	$31,627.61	September 2014	35.07%	27.18%
53.00%	$33,055.55	September 2015	49.64%	40.72%
28.83%	$51,480.00	September 2016	44.54%	35.41%
	$248,792.17			
18.89%	$5,400.00	September 2016	35.18%	26.54%
	$5,400.00			
107.25%	$25,108.59	August 2008	30.96%	24.32%
62.08%	$35,387.41		21.59%	15.63%
64.52%	$42,232.00	April 2011	26.41%	18.18%
22.96%	$39,488.00	September 2012	33.57%	23.54%
1.29%	$37,559.12	November 2013	-2.64% [2]	-9.08% [2]
28.36%	$37,455.69	January 2015	26.64%	18.62%
41.45%	$50,642.69	January 2016	19.54%	12.63%
12.18%	$45,500.00	February 2017	31.09%	21.95%
	$312,718.09			
95.95%	$19,066.00	August 2010	5.27%	0.05%
75.53%	$30,520.72	July 2011	24.50%	16.87%
60.69%	$23,385.00	July 2012	34.81%	24.74%
69.03%	$26,408.92	September 2013	7.46%	0.12%
57.71%	$50,189.85	August 2014	3.76%	-2.53%
60.20%	$49,635.00	August 2015	15.48%	8.66%
19.27%	$43,500.00	August 2016	-5.66% [1]	-11.24% [1]
	$242,705.49			
	$1,437.80		406.24%	363.78%
	$1,437.80			
	$11,271.00	November 2010	NA [13]	
	$25,485.00	July 2013		
	$29,570.50			
	$30,600.00	June 2015		
	$31,400.00			
	$128,326.50			
	$12,010.80	May 2006	24.27%	13.69%
	$13,056.90	July 2007	23.87%	16.14%
	$14,791.00	January 2008	32.95%	25.95%
	$39,858.70			
	$22,377.00	May 2006	91.05%	75.33%
	$22,377.00			
	$1,001,615.75			

APPENDIX B

1   Profit share is planned in 2017/2018, which will increase this number.

2   No profit share distribution due to not meeting contract requirements.

3   Currency conversion per www.x-rates.com.

4   Source for Philippine comparable farm gate prices: ACDI/Voca and Peter Cruz. All farm gate prices are stated at contract date.

5   Average of four sources for Ecuador comparable farm gate prices: MAGAP, ANE-CACAO, CECAO, EL UNIVERSO.

6   Currency conversion per www.xe.com.

7   Source for comparable farm gate: Convoy of Hope field technician.

8   Source for world market price is www.icco.org, and stated at the contract date. As explained in appendix A, farmers around the world do not actually receive the world market price or the Fair Trade price. Instead, they receive a fraction of that price, otherwise known as farm gate.

9   2006–2010 Fair Trade price is the world market price per metric ton + $150 per metric ton. 2011–present Fair Trade price is the world market price per metric ton + $200 per metric ton.

10   Profit share per metric ton, and profit shares in general, have fluctuated over the past ten years because we've adapted and improved how we calculate that number. In previous years we calculated it based on depletion of beans from that origin. If in one year we used more Davao beans and then used fewer beans the next year, that explains the decrease in profit share from the first year to the next. Currently, we calculate profit share based on the actual sales of those beans (turned into chocolate), so profit shares will also fluctuate based on sales of the origin.

11   This was a one-time purchase of special criollo beans.

12   This is one farm and the employees receive fair wages. Farm gate is not applicable to the wages that employees receive.

13   This is one farm and the employees receive fair wages. World market price is not applicable to the wages that employees receive.

14   This information is not applicable due to the theft of beans detailed in chapter 4.

RULE OF LIFE

My Original "Rule of Life"

Shawn Askinosie
Assumption Abbey

To the Abbot, Father Paul, Brother Francis,
and Brothers of the Community,

Why am I doing this? What do I gain? My relationship with the Abbey
started in 2001 as a guest, then as a member of the Lay Advisory
Board but this call to Family Brotherhood has been building for over
two years. The dual purposes are that I want to know God better, be in
tune, in union, in rest with the Spirit, and in so doing I hope that that
relationship will bring about the fruits of the Spirit in me: love,
kindness, gentleness, and patience. *As stated in the Message's*
rendering of Galatians 5:22–24:

22–23 But what happens when we live God's way? He brings gifts
into our lives, much the same way that fruit appears in an orchard—
things like affection for others, exuberance about life, serenity. We
develop a willingness to stick with things, a sense of compassion in the

heart, and a conviction that a basic holiness permeates things and people. We find ourselves involved in loyal commitments, not needing to force our way in life, able to marshal and direct our energies wisely.

23–24 Legalism is helpless in bringing this about; it only gets in the way. Among those who belong to Christ, everything connected with getting our own way and mindlessly responding to what everyone else calls necessities is killed off for good—crucified.

The Rule is not legalism but a guide to daily "belonging to Christ." I need particular help with this as it relates to my family and most pointedly—my wife. The practice outlined in my Rule will hopefully lead to others noticing these fruits in me. I am well aware that this "practice" will not "create" these fruits in me—that these disciplines are only pointers and signposts to what is beyond.

I pray that my Family Brotherhood at Assumption Abbey will plant the seed of community in me that will be with me wherever I go and whatever I do; especially outside the cloister. I have faith that that grace will find the still point within me where God resides and that everything else in the world—no matter the pace and apparent chaos—will revolve around it. Or as aptly stated by Father Paul—I pray for the transformation into a life of "being" inserted by "doing" and not the other way around.

[Note: This Rule was written as if it was January 1, 2015—thus the use of the present tense—but in reality it was written in October 2013.]

With God's help along with my continual turning to Christ and emptying myself as a practice I have made not only a commitment but progress in the following areas, which have collectively moved me toward "radical balance."

I PRAY: I begin each day with Lectio Divina, daily lectionary, sacred music, and short prayer. I have managed to do this almost every day. I have studied and incorporated some meditative practices of Buddhism that I can apply to my faith discipline. For myself, I daily ask God for the spirit of KINDNESS, GENTLENESS, PEACEFULNESS, and that I see the face of Christ in all who I encounter (and that they in turn see Him in me). I end every day with Examen and music.

I STUDY: I've become better acquainted with the Rule of Benedict and found ways that I can incorporate it into my life. I've worn the pages of the Benedictine Handbook. I have studied and reflected on Merton's "Bread in the Wilderness" and "Monastic Practices" by Charles Cummings. I read and reflect on the Internet Monk almost daily. I listen and reflect on the Daily Lectionary from "Pray as You Go" by Jesuit Media Initiatives. I have delved into my personal interest of the Monastic economic and "management" principle of "sufficiency." This is the idea of profit and "how much is enough?" In particular, I have incorporated some of this into my business planning. Study and reflection have always come easy to me—too easy. It's the "application to my life" part that has been a struggle. Over 2014 I've come to appreciate the contemplative benefit of the Psalms.

I ENJOY: This year I have taken time from my work to spend more time with Caron on a day trip or overnight trips to places nearby. I went to Texas to visit her family more than I did in 2013. I visit my brother and his family in L.A. at least once in 2014. I am taking time to enjoy nature on my travels to cocoa origin. I appreciate the land and have come to understand it better this year. Caron and I have made an effort to cultivate at least two good "couple" friendships. Caron and I have taken yoga and Pilates this past year and found it beneficial to our bodies. We've been doing the Five Tibetan Rites nearly every day, which has helped with our flexibility. I have learned to enjoy business travel this past year—not getting so stressed if things don't go perfectly. One thing that has helped with this is when I travel either Caron or Lawren is with me and we try to have some fun and enjoyment on the trip. I have cut back significantly in talking about work during leisure times. I have traveled to see Lawren more—just because and not for any special reason. I am more joyful and pleasant to be around b/c God has granted my prayer that I see His Son—the Christ—in everyone I encounter.

I WORK: This has been the most challenging area of balance in the past year. I've been able to pull the throttle back for a few reasons: (1) I hired a COO who has taken the "day to day" management load off my shoulders. This person has been helpful to the company but also to me. I can now travel w/o worry over tiny details back home. (2) The prayer at the start of my day combined with the surrender of my "to-do" list to God—I have peace that I've not had before. These things—more than anything else—have put years on my life.

This work/prayer/recreation balance has been "managed" and overseen by my deepening relationship to Assumption Abbey as a Family Brother. Specifically I have not taken on any additional overseas feeding programs in 2014.

The reason I have become a Family Brother is that this work/prayer/recreation balance was going to kill my relationships and me if not surrendered to God—daily. I have finally begun to understand the concept of "daily death" in ways that I did not before. I have succeeded in seeing Christ in the people I work with—my employees, my customers, and my competitors. I have a deeper understanding of the role of work in monastic life as outlined in the Rule and discussed in "Monastic Practices" by Cummings. We have a goal of [retaining our humanity while employing technology]—Cummings. Our workers are happy and not totally stressed out all of the time. Work is a path to God—hence fulfillment.

I AM HOSPITABLE: I take time during the day and night to respond to interruptions with kindness and gentleness, and an air of peacefulness. I take time to meet with friends who need me. I listen to them. I invite friends in need for coffee/tea so they will know that I am open and not too busy for them. Over the last year I have especially practiced hospitality to my wife and family. I have incorporated the Rule's importance of this practice into my study, recreation, work, and prayer.

Shawn Askinosie's Schedule

DAILY:

6:00 to 6:30 a.m.: Wake up. Listen and pray to the Daily Lectionary as found at the website Pray as You Go by Jesuit Media (http://pray-as-you-go.org/home/). The reading is three times with special sacred music. This is classic Lectio Divina. Stretching and get ready for work.

9:30 to 10:15 p.m.: Daily Examen or Ignatian breathing exercises, and stretching. Study and reflect on one of the writings mentioned above in the "I Study" section.

Meditation throughout every day: Everyone I encounter is Christ in disguise.

WEEKLY:

Noon: At least three times per week I practice Centering Prayer.

Evening: Guided prayer meditation at least two evenings per week.

Friday afternoons: I pray an end-of-week Examen.

Thursdays at 5:30 p.m.: Holy Eucharist at Christ Episcopal Church.

Sunday: I attend church when I am home and in town.

MONTHLY:

I talk on the phone with Father Paul once per month or more often if needed about my progress in keeping my Rule.

I meet with my "coach/counselor" Dan Sivils every other week to discuss my Rule.

ANNUALLY:

I travel to stay at the Abbey three times (weekends or slightly longer) in the year. The trips are in February, May/June, and October. While there I meet with Brother Francis and/or Father Paul (if present) to discuss my contemplative practice and my adherence to my Rule. I also "walk and talk" with Father Cyprian, who has been my unofficial Spiritual Director for the past thirteen years and the one who suggested that I talk to Father Paul and Brother Francis about becoming a Family Brother.

Areas of Special Accountability

- I must live a life in death and surrender so that the specific fruits of *kindness, gentleness, and peacefulness* are manifested in my daily behavior to everyone. Caron in particular needs to see this;
- I must live a life of *balance*;
- I must learn to be *present* in the here and now;

- I must learn to live an hour-by-hour life with God at the still point within me and all chaos revolving around that point; and
- I must live my life *free from the fear* of death or if not free learn to accept it in myself and make friends with it.

Father Alberic   Date
Abbot Assumption Abbey

_____

Shawn Askinosie   Date

_____

ACKNOWLEDGMENTS

Thanks to Lawren for coauthoring this book with me, for keeping me on task, on schedule, and most of all for her ability to help me articulate my ideas into coherent thoughts. To our agent, Lindsay Edgecombe, who made this a better book. To Seth Godin for being a mentor, a sounding board, and a voice of innovative reason. To my coworkers at Askinosie Chocolate, who inspire me every day: John, Kristen, Kat, Kaylyn, Flora, Ann, Dina, Gilda, Carmen, Brad, Kevin, Russell, Megan, Greg, Sara-phiner, Allison, Merry, Trevor, and Tyler. To John Cunningham, who spent hours teaching me the art and science of cash flow management. Without his counsel I might not have a business and thus would not have written this book. To Father Alberic, Father Paul, Father Cyprian, Brother Francis, and all the brothers at Assumption Abbey, who always remind me of who I am. To my great friend and lawyer, Joe Johnson, who both represents and encourages me. My thanks to Sara Carder, Heather Brennan, Brianna Yamashita, and everyone at TarcherPerigee for their hard work publishing this book. To Elsie Larson and Emma Chapman for encouraging me to write a book and tell this story. To Clay Gordon for pressure testing some assumptions, Dr. Chris Panza for teaching me non-dualism in a day, and Dr. Jody Bilyeu for reading my first rough draft. Thanks to Missy Gelner for her help in reviewing chapter 3 and making great suggestions. If I listed every person to whom I owe thanks for their encouragement during my chocolate career, this section would be longer than the book itself. But many more friends and mentors are directly mentioned and thanked in the preceding pages, like Ari and Jack.